Everything But The Kitchen Sink

a writer's memoir

Chester D. Campbell

Copyright © 2017 by Chester D. Campbell

10 9 8 7 6 5 4 3 2 1

All rights reserved. No part of this book may be used or reproduced in any manner whatsoever without the written permission of the copyright owner and Night Shadows Press.

Cover design by Stephen Walker
Printed in the United States of America

Library of Congress Control Number: 2017950550

ISBN 9780984604425

Night Shadows Press
8610 Sawyer Brown Road
Nashville, Tennessee 37221

Also by Chester D. Campbell

Suspense Novels

Hellbound

Post Cold War Political Thriller Trilogy:

Overture to Disaster (3)
The Poksu Conspiracy (2)
Beware the Jabberwock (1)

Greg McKenzie Mysteries:

A Sporting Murder (5)
The Marathon Murders (4)
Deadly Illusions (3)
Designed to Kill (2)
Secret of the Scroll (1)

Sid Chance Mysteries:

The Good, The Bad and The Murderous (2)
The Surest Poison (1)

PREFACE

THE TERM FOR this sort of book today seems to be "memoir" instead of "autobiography." The word derives from the French *memoire*, memory. That's quite appropriate as the writing requires delving into memory for a myriad of details from the past. Research is required to back up your recollections with factual data, and I was lucky in that respect, having been something of a pack rat where records and miscellanea are concerned. I have copies of military orders going back to my enlistment in the Army Reserve during World War II. I particularly enjoyed recalling my wartime experiences, which culminated in my decision to pursue a career in writing. I also have various bits of stuff from high school and junior high. My family history items include pages from an old Bible listing my mother and her siblings. Fortunately, my memory of events from the past, even way back when, remains strong. My current problem in that department involves short term memory, primarily slowness in recalling something like the name of a person, a restaurant, or a bit of information I should have written down. I usually remember it if I keep working at it.

I'll have to confess that I haven't read an autobiography in such a long time I don't remember when it was. That means I'm winging it here. I go into a lot of small details that might be left out, but I feel they help

Chester D. Campbell

round out the story of who I am. I also point out how I often used personal experiences in writing fiction. Overall, this project has been a pleasant task, although dredging up almost nine decades of personal history has been at times taxing. It has been fun recalling many of the wild things I've done in the past. This is the thirteenth book I've written, so it could be my lucky number...or an abject flop.

Chapter One

THE EARLY DAYS

I'VE READ ABOUT authors who knew writing would be their life's goal when they were quite young. Some penned stories in elementary school and gained recognition for it. But despite writing professionally for the past 70 years, I can't point to any specific incident or series of events in my early life that set me on this course. The only thing I can think of that might be relevant is my natural curiosity and my penchant for experiencing things a bit out of the ordinary. You might encounter a few of them in the following tale, which covers just shy of a century.

My earliest recollection, as best I can conclude at this late date, is of a shed behind our house. I believe it was on Mansfield Street in East Nashville. I must have been about three years old. The memory stands out like a snapshot, the edge of a wooden shed across from a garage roof. Seems like there was a gate to the alley between them. This bit of trivia makes no sense except that it helps illustrate how I got my start as something of a wanderer. I was born in the 1500 block of Fatherland Street on Monday, November 30, 1925. Must not have been much later when we moved to Mansfield, then on to 1109 Holly Street, where my first real memories began.

Before going ahead, though, I have a couple of other vague recollections to chronicle. One involved my dad driving a touring car with isinglass windows. They were thin, transparent sheets of mica, also called curtains, which could be lowered in good weather. The other dealt with an outing the family took to a town called Old Jefferson in neighboring Rutherford County. The town sat in a crook of the Stones River and was the original county seat, but it no longer exists. They demolished it after the Corps of Engineers announced plans for a dam on the river. But it was a booming area back in the late twenties when we made that trip I remember. My primary recollection involves going swimming and feeling the small rocks under my feet. I figured that's why they called it the Stones River.

The old "Monday's Child" nursery rhyme begins with "Monday's child is fair of face." I can't vouch for that, but people can't believe my age now primarily because my face isn't all wrinkled like most folks this old. Anyway, I had a fair amount of fun back then. I shared a bed with my brother Jim, two years my senior. Part of the time when we lived on Holly, my cousin Eileen Ferrell, a little younger than Jim, lived with us, as did my grandmother, Loula Catherine Wolfe Ferrell, who we lovingly called Granny. My dad, James Carl Campbell, Sr., ran a small electrical shop downtown, and my mother, Maude Ferrell Campbell, worked as a secretary at the Tennessee Inspection Bureau, which did insurance ratings. When Granny wasn't living with us, a young black woman named Bessie looked after Jim and me during the day. I've always known how to take advantage of a situation, and I would lie in bed until Bessie arrived to pull the covers down.

We romped about in the backyard in those days and passed the time in such pursuits as swinging on the front porch. I indulged in that one day I'll never forget. The street teemed with activity as workmen moved a house from around the corner. I'm a bit shady on the details, but it involved teams of horses or mules, long ropes and a capstan. With all the excitement in the street, I got the porch swing going as high as I could. The next thing I knew it flipped over and I landed on the sidewalk headfirst. That was my first experience at getting knocked out, one I would enjoy more than once in the future.

On days when the market wagon stopped in the street out front, we scooted out with Granny to survey the fresh produce as she bought groceries. When nobody was looking, we'd grab something like a pea pod and pop out the peas.

Before long we moved again, this time to 1300 Gartland Avenue, where Mom and Dad would stay until a few years after Jim and I left for Army service in World War II. I might add that in all this moving from street to street, we traveled less than a mile. The house on Gartland fit the classic definition of a bungalow, one-story with a half-width front porch. It sat between a pair of two-story-plus houses. Those tall structures turned out handy a couple of years later when the East Nashville tornado of 1933 blasted up our street but did only superficial damage to the little guy in the middle.

The location afforded me the opportunity to avoid long walks during my schooling years. Just after turning six, I entered M. M. Ross Elementary School. To get there, I could walk between the houses across the street and a short distance up the alley to where it opened onto the school grounds. Or, as my Mom made us do on most occasions, walk the block down to Fourteenth Street and a block up to Ordway, where Ross sat on the corner. Later, when I attended East Nashville Junior and Senior High schools, it was a two-block walk up to the broad swath that marked the beginning of Gallatin Pike. The schools sat facing the thoroughfare that would take you all the way to Gallatin, some thirty miles to the northeast.

Having a smart brother paving the way had its drawbacks. On more than one occasion the teacher took me into the cloakroom, a small caged area where coats and such were hung, and chastised me for not being as good as my older sibling. But I fared a lot better than the first grade boy the teacher frequently found peeing in his chair. Maybe he had an aversion to using the outdoor privy, which employed a long trough in the floor for such deeds. When it came time for recess, the schoolyard reverberated with the raucous sounds of kids at play. That included occasional bouts of juvenile fisticuffs over some minor disagreement. I normally avoided such playfulness in favor of the company of the fairer sex. In those days the school system operated on two separate semesters in which the grades were identified as Low and High. Six-year-olds with birthdays like mine started school in the middle of the year. We would be High First Grade in the fall. When they went to a standard fall-spring calendar a couple of years later, they bumped up my class half a year to the next grade. It made me graduate from high school at age 17.

I mentioned the tornado of 1933. It occurred on the evening of March 14. I remember it being quite warm and still that afternoon when school let out. In fact, it was in the upper 70s, unusual for mid-March. We had been listening to some mystery radio program like *Chandu the Magician* early in the evening, and the old Atwater Kent that sat on the living room table began to crackle with static. The storm hit on the west side of town around 7:30, then blasted through downtown, crossed the Cumberland River and wreaked havoc on East Nashville. Later estimated as an F3 tornado, it widened to 800 yards and killed eleven people on our side of town. It may be a cliché, but I recall it sounding like a locomotive as it roared up the street. Bricks fell down the chimney into the fireplace, and Dad rushed us down the stairs into the basement. The roof leaked, and when he was sure the storm had left, he herded us out to the garage and into the car for the drive over to my aunt Rosie's house, which the storm had missed. By then it was pouring rain by the bucketsful and the backyard resembled a pond.

My life on Gartland soon became spiced-up by other kids on the street. The Greens moved in next door with two boys and two girls. Johnny, the oldest, who was a year older than me, became my best buddy in those serene days of youth. Mary Frances, called "Faffy," a year younger than me, turned out to be my first crush. Mary Greenwood, about the same age as Faffy, lived down the street. These were the core of our playtime group, although the younger Green daughter, Dot, would soon come along. We enjoyed such typical kid's games as hopscotch, kick the can, and red rover.

As we got a little older and received bicycles for Christmas, they became our principle mode of transportation. Not the best businessman around, Dad had to skimp and cut corners wherever possible. My first bike was a patchwork job with big blobs where parts had been welded together. Johnny and I pulled such spoofs as telling our mothers we were spending the night with the other one. The Greens lived in their grandfather's home, and he had a garage in back of the big residence. Some nights we would climb up on the flat roof of the garage and lie there watching the stars. Occasionally, around two a.m., we would ride our bikes up to Gallatin Pike and lay on the pavement in front of the Carnegie

Library Branch that occupied the "V" shape where Eleventh Street and Main Street came together to form Gallatin Pike. At that time of night back then, only one vehicle an hour might come by.

In the early days, Mr. Green sold packaged peanut butter and crackers. He hired women who worked in the "Little House," a small one-room structure beside the garage, slathering peanut butter on crackers. Later he cleaned out the place, and Johnny and I used it as a play house. We built model airplanes, which we brought in and talked about being pilots when we grew up. Using a world map that likely came from one of our parents' *National Geographic* magazines, we plotted flights around the globe.

Johnny and I were thrilled no end at the news of Wrong Way Corrigan's small plane flight from New York to Ireland in the summer of 1938. My interest was piqued further by my father's habit of driving out to Berry Field, the Nashville airport, on Sunday afternoons to watch the planes take off and land. That same summer he bought tickets and took my brother Jim and me for a ride in an Ogden Tri-Motor. Jim and I shared a room at the back of the house, and during that time we scrounged pieces of wood and built the framework for a semblance of an airplane cockpit in our room.

Johnny's uncle, Allison Trice, further whetted our appetite for flying. A member of the Air National Guard's 105th Observation Squadron, he took us to the airport and let us climb in one of their O-47s. It was a squat, single-engine airplane that sat low on the ramp. It had a long greenhouse-type canopy. I used one in the plot of *The Marathon Murders*. I had no thought back in those early days that I might some day be a member of the same outfit, though its name and mission had changed.

Everything But The Kitchen Sink

    The memory is a little hazy after 77 years, but it likely occurred the summer after I turned fourteen that Johnny Green and I made a little money selling magazines such as *The Saturday Evening Post* and *Liberty*. A magazine sales rep would park his car at the curb, and us kids gathered around. He doled out the magazines, and we wandered about the neighborhood selling them door-to-door. He paid us five or ten cents per copy sold. We saved our nickels and dimes with a plan in mind. On trips to the airport with our parents, we had seen a sleek WACO biplane with a snazzy radial engine and streamlined fenders over the wheels, piloted by a smiling young man with a windblown look. He sold 30-minute joy rides for five dollars. We had pedaled our bikes all over the East Nashville area and knew our way around. Sneaking a map from one of our parents' cars, we plotted our route to the airport about ten miles away. Using our normal excuse, he told his mother he intended to go somewhere with me, and I told my grandmother, who kept us while my mother worked, that I planned on going somewhere with Johnny.

    With our $2.50 each in our pockets and small brown bags of peanut butter and crackers, plus a couple of candy bars, we embarked on our journey. Rather than head south toward town, we rode north to the Inglewood suburb where the McGavock Pike ferry (which closed in 1965) took us across the river. From there, we only had to follow McGavock to the airport. We had picked a bright, sunny day and encountered no problems along the way. The trip took a couple of hours. After resting up a bit while we ate our goodies, we headed over to the fence area where the pilot hung out. Security precautions didn't exist in those days. We showed him our cash and said we were ready to ride. I think he would have preferred $5 each, but the plane was a two-seater, and we would only occupy one seat together. He led us out the ramp to where the plane sat.

We hadn't left the ground, but we were flying high. He boosted us into the open cockpit and strapped us down. A little prop cranking to start the engine, and we were off into the wild blue yonder. It gave us the most exhilarating feeling you can imagine. He did some steep turns so we could see the landscape below. I think he looped it, but I wouldn't swear to that. This happened around 1939, before the FAA came around to complicate things. The thirty minutes ended all too soon. With that thrilling experience to chatter about, we didn't start worrying until we got close to home. "Where have you been?" our keepers demanded as soon as we arrived. We admitted to crossing the river and peddling around McGavock Pike, but nothing about the airport. Things remained pretty tense for awhile.

During this time our backyard could have been renamed Campbell Field. All the boys in the neighborhood flocked in to play football in the fall. Jim and I sometimes used it to our advantage. Dad always kept an eye out for the latest electrical devices, and he had installed a stoker to feed coal into the furnace automatically. But hauling cinders out of the furnace required two boys, not some automatic device. Occasionally we would boost an old washtub full of cinders up to the basement window and get waiting football players to carry them out to the alley. When the game started, we didn't indulge in something simple like touch football. We played tackle, and it made you run like hell when you had the ball. I enjoyed it enough that I decided to go out for football when I got to high school. That's another story.

As I mentioned earlier, I experienced my first infatuation with Johnny's sister, Faffy. That probably occurred around age ten. Many others would follow as I've never had a problem with falling in love, though when the real thing showed up it lasted a long time. When I got into junior high, I fell in love with one of Faffy's friends, Marge Hargrove, who I met at the Green's house. I had never been the outgoing type and was rather bashful as well. I would bring her packs of chewing gum at school and chat in the corridors or on the lawn at lunchtime. During warm weather when sunset came late, I would walk to her street, several blocks away, and stroll past her house hoping she might appear at the door. She never did. I used that experience for a character in one of my novels. Marge went on to marry a neurosurgeon.

In high school I got a little bolder with a girl named Dottie Wechsel. I carried her books as I walked her home some eight or ten blocks past where I lived. We would sit on the porch and talk, and I got to know her mother quite well. She worked downtown at a telephone answering service. I wound up doing better with the mother than the daughter. My problem: I had little money and hadn't reached the age for a driver's license. A guy with his own car soon swept her away. But I used her last name for a character in *A Sporting Murder*.

My senior year I fell for a girl who attended East End Methodist Church, where I had belonged since birth. Her dad, a preacher assigned to the district office, soon moved to a church a few miles away in Northeast Nashville. I had to take a bus to First Street, on the east side of the river opposite downtown, then transfer to another bus to reach Ruth Johnson's house. Standing there waiting for the second bus, I got a generous dose of the soot that settled out of the coal-burning pollution of the central business district in those days, a smoky pall parodied by the morning newspaper with a cartoon character called "Smoky Joe." My white shirt wound up with black specks. Ruth and I dated until I went into the Army in World War II, and the few times I got home after that. But when the war ended, I went off to college in Knoxville and she went her way back home. I used some of our experiences while writing about characters in my suspense novel *Hellbound*.

I suppose falling in love will always be fashionable, and we'll get to more of that later, but let's get back to those early days. One of eight children, my mother had been closest to the next to oldest of her siblings, Rose Ferrell, for as long as I could remember. Us kids called her Rosie. I don't know why, but my brother and I always called my mother's brothers and sisters by their first names but applied Aunt or Uncle to Dad's siblings. Rosie never married–an old maid as they were called back then. She lived near us, and she considered me her favorite nephew, so I got plenty of attention. During the week she taught piano and played music for a county elementary school named Rosemont. My grandfather, Alfred Elmore Douglass Ferrell, was a teacher and principal and a force in education in the part of the county once called Flatrock. Born in 1858, he died before I came along. He gave Rosemont school its name. He also gave me my middle name, Douglas, minus the final "s." On Sundays Rosie played the pipe organ at East End Methodist Church on Holly Street. My brother Jim and I had to take piano lessons from her, and she wanted to teach me to play the organ. A kid who had rather play outside and hated to practice, I turned down the organ lessons, much to my later regret. I did learn to play the piano, though, and enjoyed it for many years. I was never good at sight reading but memorized my favorite songs. My prowess, or lack thereof, came into play a few years later.

Our family traveled a lot by auto in those days. Some of our more memorable ventures involved visiting my Mom's sisters. We headed up U.S.41 in 1934 when it hardly resembled a highway by today's standards, with a destination of Chicago, then home to my aunt Estelle and her husband, Wade Grey, plus Mom's oldest brother, Frank Ferrell, and his wife, Annie Kate. We arrived there in time for the final year of the Century of Progress World's Fair. I don't remember a lot about the fair, except for the Sky Ride with its cars that cruised high above the fairgrounds, plus the Midway with its mean-looking dragon ride that circled around the tracks. While I found the fair quite entertaining, the thing that stands out most about Chicago took place on the day we played with uncle Frank's daughters and I got hit in the nose with a ball. I still have a bone that sticks out slightly on one side of my nose.

I must not have been much older when we traveled to Texas to visit another of my mother's sisters, Marguerite, who lived in San Antonio with her husband, Howard Winans. This marked another chapter in my fascination with aviation. Howard worked as an aircraft mechanic at Kelly Field, one of the oldest U.S. air bases, and he took us there to see the shops where they worked on aircraft. I'll never forget going into the paint shop where they applied dope, a plasticised lacquer, to the fabric covering of the planes. The smell penetrated everything. The odor made it seem like you were standing in a pool of mashed bananas.

Another memorable trip took place when we visited my great uncle Ned Wolfe, who had a large farm outside St. Augustine, Florida. We arrived in the St. Augustine area one day around dusk. Highways were not well marked in those days, and as we drove along, Dad suddenly slammed on the brakes. The road ended where the dark waters of the Atlantic Ocean lapped up near our car. Scared me to death. We spent about a week at Uncle Ned's, visiting the Fountain of Youth, the old fort called Castillo de San Marcos, and other tourist spots. One sight I remember from that venture took place on a pond in back of the house, where a lone crane would appear every morning standing just inside the water.

    I got my first job around the summer of 1939 when I was thirteen years old. I earned twelve-and-a-half cents an hour delivering orders on my bicycle for J.P. Brown Drug Store on Gallatin Pike near East High. Sometimes it required riding all the way out to the Inglewood suburb. In later summers, Dad worked Jim and me at his electrical shop. My first memory of the business was at a location on Fourth Avenue South just beyond Demonbreun Street, where the Country Music Hall of Fame and Museum now stands. Later he moved around the corner on Demonbreun, which is currently part of the Music City Walk of Fame Park. The work was right up Jim's alley. He later became an electrical engineer and headed Nashville Electric Service's engineering department. I, on the other hand, did not like getting my hands dirty, as Mom would point out with raised eyebrows on more than one occasion. I still have one of Dad's advertising pencils with J. C. Campbell Company on it, the address and phone number. I called it so many times I can still remember it–52301.

    I had several jobs in my teen years which did little to prepare me for my eventual vocation. They included selling women's shoes at a small store on Third Avenue just off the Public Square, gathering work clothes to fill orders at Washington Manufacturing Company on Second Avenue, and sorting mail at the Main Post Office (now the Frist Center for the Visual Arts) for Army units on maneuvers in Middle Tennessee. That shoe store job was the most harrowing. Squeezing some of the feet women wanted to shove into too small shoes was ridiculous.

Looking back, my high school years seem rather unremarkable. I mentioned earlier about going out for football. What a disaster. The first day we dressed out for a scrimmage, my mouth collided with some guy's knee, and most of the tooth next to my upper middle teeth landed on the playing field. I turned in my uniform, knowing what would happen when Mom came home from work. She looked at my mouth and said my football days were over. A few years earlier I had fallen in the neighbor's driveway, breaking my two upper front teeth into an inverted "V" shape. After my unfortunate football experience, the dentist decided to pull all four front teeth and replace them with a fixed bridge. In those days, dentists only used Novocain when pulling teeth, but by then I had a mouth full of fillings that had provided more than enough experience with the torments of low-speed drills.

Fortunately, my other choices for livening up my high school days went much better. I took part in a smattering of student activities, many in minor roles. Instead of playing a significant part in a play, I helped build sets for the Dramatic Guild. I found the Spanish Club interesting because I enjoyed learning the language. I studied two years in high school and another in college but never learned to speak the language. In later years I remembered enough to make out signs in Spanish when we traveled out West, and even now I frequently run into familiar Spanish words. But the subjects that I enjoyed most lay in the science field, taught by my favorite high school teacher, Miss Roberta Kirkpatrick. In another area, I played an active role in the Junior Civitan Club and in my senior year was a member of the Student Council. I served on the staff of *The Grey Eagle*, our student annual, but had nothing to do with the writing. I canvassed the area as an advertising salesman. That, I should point out, became a job I inherited several years later when I started *Nashville Magazine*.

My most significant extracurricular activity in high school, one which would serve me well after graduation, came with participation in Junior ROTC (Reserve Officer Training Corps). I signed on in the tenth grade and moved ahead in the ranks each year. The unit was organized as a battalion. I wore captain's bars as a senior and served as the battalion's adjutant. Our battalion commander, Major G. C. Fitzgerald, became one of 58 East High students who died in World War II. Another eighteen hundred of us served. In my junior year, I received the Overall Medal as the outstanding ROTC cadet in Nashville. Don't ask why.

I've always been a joiner. Taking part in various groups has been my practice for many years. In fact, promoting organization membership became a major part of my job as an association executive, the profession I followed for eighteen years before retirement. In all that time, I hadn't let myself get too close to people. My only life-long friend is one I acquired during those high school days, Dan Leech. Dan and I palled around and did some crazy things, particularly after he got his driver's license. I remember one day when we cruised up the street and Dan swung the steering wheel, letting the car spin around in the street. We made sure there were no other vehicles in sight. His dad would have murdered him if he'd known about it. We did some worthwhile things, too. I think it was in the twelfth grade that Miss Kirkpatrick taught an aeronautics class. Dan and I and another friend built a wind tunnel that we entered in a science fair. I don't recall if we won any awards, but I have an 8x10 of us posing with our project. Dan was a year older than me, but he had some family medical issues that caused him to be held back a year in school. Toward the end of our senior year, in the spring of 1943, a lot of the guys signed up in the reserves with call-up dates after graduation. Dan and I were among those who chose the Army Air Forces aviation cadet program.

Chapter Two

WORLD WAR II

I HAD TURNED seventeen the past November when I volunteered for service in the Army Air Forces in the late spring of 1943. When the recruiting sergeant asked, "When do you want to go on active duty?" I said December first, the day after my eighteenth birthday. He reminded me that would be just before Christmas and told me I didn't want to go then. With all the guys I knew headed for the war, I was ready to go. But I agreed to wait until January sixth. I'm an inveterate minutia keeper, and I still have nearly all of my military records, including the orders on my enlistment giving me an Army serial number, which I can repeat even now. My next orders came December 31, 1943 directing me to proceed on January 6, 1944 to Camp Shelby, near Hattiesburg, Mississippi, for official entry into the service.

Mom and Ruth saw me off at Union Station, the big downtown depot where multiple tracks led off to parts unknown. With the lack of passenger trains in recent years, the structure has been transformed into the Union Station Hotel. But on that cold day 73 years ago, huge locomotives huffed and puffed and let off clouds of steam as they waited below the metal staircase we walked down after purchasing my ticket. I boarded the train for Memphis, where I would change trains for the Mississippi leg of the journey. On the way I met a few of my fellow to-be-cadets who I would continue to encounter during my Army career, if that is the proper term.

Camp Shelby turned out to be a muddy hell hole. We were issued uniforms and ordered around by a garrulous first sergeant who taught me a new word. When he threatened us with dire consequences should we disobey his orders, he emphasized it with, "I'll guaran-damn-tee you'll regret it!" I used that for a character in one of my novels. It proved just part of the indoctrination into Army ways. But as bad as we found Camp Shelby, our orders sending us there contained a silver lining. The other neophyte soldiers didn't believe us when we told them in a few days we'd be heading to Miami Beach.

We basked in the warm sunshine of South Florida, location of one of several Army Air Forces Basic Training centers. If you have to take Basic, that's the place to do it. I was assigned a room on the fourth floor of a hotel on Collins Avenue, a block off the ocean front. Read that "beach." But we only got to see the beach on weekends. Most of the time we did things like run up and down several flights of steps to get into formation. Elevators were off limits. We spent our days marching back and forth to a nearby golf course where we sat on the ground and listened to instructors. We learned all the usual Army stuff like how to handle weapons, the eleven General Orders for guard duty, and they threw in one segment to remind us that the Army sometimes stalks and shoots folks. We carried our rifles and moved furtively on a mission through a field of palmetto plants whose spiny tips speared our arms and legs when we got too close. They also put us on guard duty with our ammunition-less rifles. I spent most of one night walking around an ordinary-looking building in Miami that showed no evidence of a military connection. The Air Forces side of

Basic included a battery of tests designed to determine our qualifications for training as pilots, bombardiers, or navigators. Some of us only qualified for one or two, but I managed to be among those who could go into any of the aircrew slots.

Basic Training soon ended, and they loaded us onto a train to Valdosta, Georgia, where we took up residence at Moody Field. This was around the first of March in 1944. Moody was equipped with twin-engine AT-10 aircraft used to train pilots for duty on bombers or other multi-engine aircraft. We envied those aviation cadets out on the flight line, but I suspect all of us wannabe pilots harbored visions of flying fighter aircraft. That appeared somewhere out in the future, however, for my contingent of would-be aviation cadets received the title of On-the-Line Trainees (OLTs). Google provided an insight into this decision, directing me to Chapter 17 of *The Army Air Forces in World War II*. Requests for aircrews in combat theaters declined sharply as the air war went our way. This resulted in a slowdown in the progression of cadets through the training program and the creation of large pools of people like me left in limbo. The AAF put the OLT program into effect in February 1944, just in time to send me to Moody.

The history stated the Training Command advised that "trainees will be given duty assignments with aircraft maintenance and servicing where they will get more practical training for their future instruction." Our practical training consisted of things like raking gravel in front of the headquarters building. We were also told we had to help build a firing range because German prisoners of war refused to work on the project. I had seen some of the POWs going through the chow line while I did a shift on KP, an additional practical training assignment. I sat around tinkering with a piano in the recreation area one day when a guy involved in putting together a band asked if I'd like to join them. I thought what the heck, why not? That is until we sat down to practice and I faced sight-reading a stack of sheet music. Not my forte. I bluffed my way through, hitting enough correct notes to sound like I knew what I was doing. It didn't last long before we got orders to ship out.

Another wrinkle put in the program to slow the progression of future aircrew trainees, and to provide people like us recent high school graduates with more education, involved something called the College Training Detachment. That became my next destination after Moody Field. Our train trip from southern Georgia took us to Rock Hill, South Carolina, where we reported to our CTD commander at Winthrop College—an all-girl institution at that time. This was a novel experience, but they kept us busy and fairly well segregated from the school girls. The program originally lasted ten weeks but by now had been cut almost in half. The academics included math, physics, current history, geography, English, and civil air regulations. It was enough to provide me with a few hours of credit when I enrolled at the University of Tennessee. One interesting feature that has wound up haunting me in recent months was ten hours of pilot training in a Piper Cub. We rode out to the local airport and took turns getting one-hour lessons, sometimes twice a day. Among the records I kept from the war I found my pilot's log from the Rock Hill airport. I logged seven hours between June 11 and June 22, 1944. Then, while waiting our turns, a few of us got playful, as eighteen-year-olds will do, and I started turning cartwheels. I hit the second toe on my right foot against a rock and toppled to the ground in pain. They took me to a military hospital in Charlotte where they bandaged my swollen foot and gave me a pair of crutches. That ended my flying career, but I got off the crutches a couple of weeks later in time for our departure to Shaw Field at Sumter, South Carolina.

I found myself back in the OLT routine and life in an Army barracks. At first it was the same old story, KP and seemingly useless chores. Then I got lucky. I don't remember how it happened, but I got chosen to work in the Air Inspector's office. They assigned me to the mundane task of filing Army Regulations in an array of books. My superiors probably thought I had drawn a boring job, but they weren't aware of my insatiable desire to soak up any kind of knowledge, a habit that has helped in my fiction writing. One of the inspection office's main jobs was checking on aircraft maintenance. The base housed a large basic flying training school for both American and French cadets. I soon made the acquaintance of a young lieutenant in the office who flew the BT-13 Vultee "Vibrator" trainers for a check flight after a major engine overhaul. He let me ride in the student seat several times. Once when I got a three-day pass, I met Mom and Ruth in Atlanta. My memories about that trip center around our visit to see a movie at the fabulous Fox Theatre. Its ornate interior complete with twinkling stars in the "sky" above looked awesome. Music from the massive theater organ made it even more dazzling. The Fox had been in existence only fifteen years at the time. It closed as a movie theater in 1974 and has since been reincarnated as a performing arts center.

After seven-plus months of on-the-line training at Shaw Field, I finally received orders appointing me an aviation cadet and directing me to proceed to the San Antonio Aviation Cadet Center (called SAACC, as in "sack") for preflight training. SAACC, currently known as Lackland Air Force Base, was located next to Kelly Field, which I had visited back about age ten with my uncle Howard Winans, a visit that still lingered in my mind because of the overwhelming odor of dope being applied to aircraft fabric. Of course, airplanes by now were covered with aluminum, not fabric.

Preflight proved to be a mixture of military instruction and academic courses heavy on the aeronautical aspect. For the military part, we spent hours in close order drill, ceremonies, and inspections, stuff I was familiar with from high school ROTC. We also "enjoyed" lots of calisthenics and other forms of physical training. And we received such interesting instruction as familiarization with chemical warfare defense, where we sat in a room with gas masks on while a gas was pumped in. Another was high altitude simulation where we sat in a cubicle with oxygen masks on while the chamber was depressurized. We removed our masks momentarily to experience the lack of oxygen. The classroom subjects included things like target identification, meteorology, reading aeronautical maps and charts and using them in solving operational problems. We had to learn the Morse code, and they used slides to teach us to recognize enemy aircraft instantly.

Sundays during that ten weeks of preflight were spent around San Antonio. I visited my aunt a few times, and I joined some buddies on dates. I recall one weekend I dated a general's daughter. Don't remember how that came about. One guy had a car and we picked her up at the general's quarters. On another occasion we went to Brackenridge Park, on the creek-like San Antonio River, where they gave free rattlesnake sandwiches on weekends. I declined. They said it tasted like chicken.

Chester D. Campbell

I thought the end of preflight would bring assignment to basic flying school. Wrong. Preflight Class 245 finished in May of 1945 and I, along with a contingent of my fellow cadets, traveled just east of San Antonio to Randolph Field, known as the "West Point of the Air." It proved another delay because flying training had been cut back, and there was no room for us. But Randolph turned out to be an intriguing experience. One of the earliest U.S. air bases, opened in 1930, it's square design included concentric circular streets in the center with runways on three sides. The installation had been enlarged by the time I got there, but it's permanent buildings stood out with their Spanish Colonial architecture featuring arched openings and red tile roofs, hardly like any other air base I've ever seen.

Randolph had ceased its flying training role in 1943, now only training instructor pilots, those who already had their wings. I managed to experience another organization it hosted, the School of Aviation Medicine, which trained flight surgeons. They assigned us the job of guinea pigs for the school. We got poked and probed in practice physical exams, and we took part in drug tests. I remember one where we took an airsickness pill, waited awhile, then climbed into a gondola attached to a bar set up like a swing. They kept it swinging higher and higher, faster and faster, until the rider got sick. I finally did, although I've never been sick on an airplane. Maybe I got the placebo.

After several weeks, they assigned us jobs around the base, just like the old on-the-line training days. My luck held and I became one of two clerks for the transient officers' quarters. Another cadet named Wolfson joined me. Our job involved checking the officers in and out, mostly aircrew members in for a short stay. We had an office and a room where we slept. We took turns at another task, serving as cashier for the Officers Mess, located on the floor below the transient quarters. That's where we ate as well. Most days weren't too busy, so we had plenty of time to ourselves. While chatting, I learned that Wolfson had finished a year at Yale before joining the service.

"If I had it to do over again," he said one day, "I'd study journalism."

That subject had never entered my mind before, but it somehow resonated with me. I guess Mom was right–it was a way I could use my hands without getting them dirty. Whatever, it marked the start of my pursuit of a writing career. It also led to my efforts at fiction writing. We had a typewriter in the office, an old Underwood, and I sat down one day, cranked in a sheet of paper, and started banging out a story that had just entered my head. This came right after the atomic bomb had decimated Hiroshima. I let my imagination run wild and began writing a story dealing with nuclear weapons. I didn't get far with it–which was a good thing since I knew little about the subject–because the war soon ended. But it gave birth to that little voice down deep inside that pops up when you least expect it, a voice that would bug me over the years with the idea of writing fiction.

With the war ended, my aviation cadet colleagues began fretting over rumors the Army planned to kick us back to buck privates and ship us to Japan for the occupation. Another rumor I heard said some of the cadets had papas with influence in Washington. At any rate, by early October they told us to start processing out. That meant standing in line, going from one station to another, getting all our records together, getting paid. We also endured a medical check where we were asked

Chester D. Campbell

if we had any service-connected problems. When I told them about my broken toe, they said I'd have to be examined at the base hospital to get it on my records. Otherwise I'd have no basis for a claim later with the Veterans Administration. I didn't want any delays in getting out of there, so I said no thanks.

Chapter Three

THE COLLEGE YEARS

On OCTOBER 29, 1945, with discharge orders in hand, I bummed a ride on a C-46 to Brookley Field at Mobile, Alabama. From there I took a train to Nashville. Home again, I looked around for what to do with my future. I wanted to study journalism, but I had no idea where. Brother Jim had finished a year at the University of Tennessee before going into the Army, and I followed him as usual with an application to UT. I signed up for a generic academic program, figuring I could check on journalism schools before my sophomore year. I headed to Knoxville via Greyhound in January 1946 and got a room near the campus with a friend from church also taking advantage of the GI Bill. Our landlady could be described best as a frumpy woman. We dubbed her "Messie Bessie" after a cartoon character. Receiving a solid academic background in high school, I had no trouble with my start in college. At the end of the spring quarter, I headed back home and found my buddy Dan Leech, who had wound up as an Army Air Forces navigator, also out of the service. Being interested in engineering, he joined me in the college quest.

In my research I had found two universities in the middle section of the country with renowned journalism schools–Wisconsin and Missouri. We started out taking a bus to the edge of town on U.S. 41 and stuck out our thumbs. After a decent interval, a car stopped and we jumped in. This was a time before people feared hitchhikers or hitchhiking. The jovial driver asked where we were headed and proceeded to take us all the way to Chicago. We soon made it to Madison and checked out the University of Wisconsin. Dan didn't find what he was looking for, though the journalism school appeared fine to me. The program began with the junior year, leaving me plenty of time to decide.

We hitchhiked our way home in time for me to enroll in the summer quarter at UT. In addition to the normal twelve-week session, summer school provided two six-week segments that involved daily classes in a subject rather than the usual three days a week. My schedule was a mish-mash of all three: English and history the first six weeks, economics and Spanish the second six weeks, and Chemistry for the entire twelve weeks. It was enough to complete my freshman year and make me a sophomore in the fall. I also took a correspondence course in French which I completed in September.

As more veterans flooded onto the campus thanks to the GI Bill, housing became a problem. The university threw up a row of temporary wooden buildings that meandered down Fifteenth Street along the bottom of a hill. The main campus was called "The Hill," and it provided a steep climb to get to class. The housing location had its good side though, being just across the street from Ellis and Ernest Drugstore, called E&E, which served as the main student hangout and the place where I had breakfast every morning, such as it was. The new dormitory buildings featured small rooms with two beds and a corridor that ran along in front of them. Dan and I snagged one.

When I checked the course list for the next quarter, lo and behold I found a journalism class. I signed up for it immediately. Turned out it was taught by Steve

Humphrey, who took a year's sabbatical from his job as associate editor of *The Knoxville Journal* and decided to be a teacher of a basic reporting course. As a journalist in the making, I signed on with the biweekly student newspaper, *The Orange and White.* I moved up in the ranks quickly. By the end of my sophomore year, I had been chosen to take over as managing editor for one of the two weekly editions. Fate, however, or the machinations of a newspaper editor, would change that.

When summer came, Dan and I were still looking for another school. I had found that the University of Missouri had one of the top-rated journalism schools. One of Dan's relatives had died and left him an A-Model Ford. I don't remember but I think it was a 1928 coupe. We set off in it for Columbia, Missouri. Along the way, we noticed something red beneath a crack in the floorboard on the passenger side. We pulled to the side of the road and found a red hot exhaust manifold. From then on we checked the radiator frequently and carried a bottle of water to top it off. During our time at the University of Missouri, we stopped by the Lambda Chi Alpha house to visit our brothers in the fraternity we had joined during the past school year. I liked what I learned about the journalism school, but it would be more expensive since I'd be an out-of-state student.

When I got the fall quarter information from UT, surprisingly it showed a full-blown School of Journalism had been created in the College of Business Administration under Professor Willis Tucker. In addition to his teaching experience, Prof Tucker had served reporting and editing stints with the Beckley, West Virginia *Evening Post,* the Lexington *Herald-Leader*, and WGAR in Cleveland, Ohio. I wouldn't need to transfer to another school after all. Dan's A-Model served as our transportation to the Knoxville campus, and during trips back and forth we did such silly tricks as driving at night up U.S. 70 with the lights off when a bright moon illuminated the road ahead. Of course, we encountered hardly any traffic late at night. On arriving in Knoxville at the end of the summer, I learned something quite exciting. Our old journalism teacher had decided to hire some of his former students as reporters for *The Knoxville Journal*. I went in to see Steve Humphrey and he hired me on the spot, at the enormous salary of $50 a week. He knew we couldn't earn more than that without cutting into our GI Bill benefits. That didn't matter to me, elated over being an honest-to-God daily newspaper reporter instead of managing editor of a student publication. I had to adjust my class schedule since I would be going to work in the afternoon and getting off around eleven or twelve at night. *The Journal* published in the morning. I also needed to buy a car to get back and forth to work. Mom, ever my most staunch supporter, advanced me enough money to pay for a used Plymouth Valiant.

Brother Jim had married his high school sweetheart while home on furlough before going overseas to Okinawa, and he had come back to UT since his discharge. He and his wife, Anita, lived in temporary married student housing on the other side of the campus. I visited them a few times, but not often. Carrying thirteen hours of classes and working eight hours at the newspaper kept me quite busy. But I managed. Dan dropped out of school and I moved into a basement room in the Lambda Chi Alpha fraternity house, a jumbo-sized old residence just off campus on Temple Avenue, now Volunteer Boulevard. I didn't realize that cub reporters, as we were called, started strictly at the bottom of the pecking order. I wrote obituaries, which involved taking the list of deaths, calling the funeral homes and getting all the details. If I identified the corpse as somebody newsworthy, it meant going to the newspaper library and digging into the files. Before long I got assignments to cover outside stories. I still have the edition with my first by-line packed away somewhere in the attic. The story involved a dog show.

That little voice down deep inside popped up around this time and the fiction bug snuck out. Whenever I had some spare time, mostly on my days off from *The Journal*, I sat at my little portable typewriter in my room at the fraternity house and pecked out a novel titled "Time Waits for Murder." A murder mystery, it featured a–guess what–newspaper reporter. The first chapter bore the title "Murder, He Wrote." Shades of Jessica Fletcher. I sent it to a publisher and got it back promptly with a stock rejection slip. I stuck the fiction bug into the little voice and slipped it back down deep inside my psyche.

On one of my journeys back home, I served as best man at Dan Leech's wedding. He subsequently brought his bride to Knoxville and finished what he had started earlier.

At the newspaper I soon moved up to more interesting assignments. But during the first part of the day I concentrated on subjects like math, Spanish, writing feature articles, practicum in journalism, and military science. The latter meant Air ROTC, which I took because I decided if I had to go back into the military I wasn't going to be an enlisted man. During the summer at the end of that school year my AFROTC class went to summer camp at Keesler Air Force Base near Biloxi, Mississippi. One of my classmates was a friend from Nashville who had lived on the next street over from my house. He had been in some rough fighting in Europe during the war. He never talked about it, but a year after graduation it finally got to him and he committed suicide. That was before PTSD and all the efforts at rehabilitation.

I had cut back on my class hours during that first year after going to work at *The Journal*, but I returned to a full schedule for my senior year. I never came close to being a straight A student like my brother Jim or my little brother Howard, who came along eleven years after me and attended bitter rival Vanderbilt. However, I did have a decent B-minus average. In June 1949 I graduated in Business Administration with a major in journalism. That left me concerned only with my fulltime job at *The Knoxville Journal*. Better assignments came my way now, such as interviewing congressmen and senators. I don't want to do a disservice to anyone's memory, but one interview that stands out involved either a silver-haired congressman from Upper East Tennessee or, more likely, a Memphis senator. The gentleman started talking as soon as I introduced myself and didn't stop until I folded my note pad and departed.

Chapter Four

THE KOREAN WAR

On June 25, 1950, 75,000 North Korean soldiers stormed across the 38th parallel into South Korea, and the Korean War began. At the time, I had been a second lieutenant in the Air Force Reserve for just over a year, since graduation from UT. I had been assigned to the Knoxville reserve group, which offered little activity, but I learned that an Air National Guard unit had begun the process of formation. It had an opening for an intelligence officer, a job that fit me like a pair of fur-lined gloves. Uncovering information somebody wanted to keep secret happened to be one big thing I loved about the newspaper business. I figured that's what intelligence officers did. As I learned later, I was partially right.

    I joined the 119th Aircraft Control & Warning Squadron of the Tennessee Air National Guard, which met at the National Guard Armory in Knoxville. Its radar sets were quite a novelty back then, small screens that showed blips giving the location of aircraft in range. We met one weekend a month, and I had little to do in my official capacity. Meanwhile, at work I had plenty to do. I wrote different kinds of stories, including one where I rode out into the countryside with a photographer to cover the crash of a small airplane. On the way back, we crested a hill and almost ran into a motorcycle wreck that had obviously just occurred. We got out and walked over to see the most gory sight I had ever witnessed. Two men lay there, blood flowing onto the pavement. One of them had been impaled by the handlebar of the motorcycle, a scene I will never forget, one that has kept me from riding a motorcycle ever since.

I did general assignments for a while, covering whatever came across the city editor's desk. I did a stint on the police beat, then shifted to the city hall beat. That work on the police beat started a different story that lasted nearly fifty years. One facet of that assignment involved daily visits to the emergency room at Knoxville General Hospital, where any medical event that might have been interesting to the cops or newspaper reporters wound up. The nurses kept a register of every patient, what brought them to the ER, etc. Reporters were interested in gunshot wounds, car wrecks, that sort of thing. We also took time to chat with the nurses. I met an attractive student nurse named Alma Miracle who I took a fancy to. I learned that she had an older sister, Carrie, in the same nursing class. They had a sister older than Carrie named Bonnie, who had already graduated and was a Registered Nurse working at another hospital. The girls' parents had died, but they had a brother younger than Alma, Ira, and a brother older than Bonnie named Roy. Bill Keel, a fellow journalism student who I had shared an apartment with during our last year at UT, dated another student in the Miracle sisters' class, Jean Harmon.

I dated Alma a few times as a student, and after she got her wings, her RN designation, that is, we became an item. She and Carrie found hospital jobs and moved into a small house on Gratz Street, just off North Broadway. I spent time with her at home after work. On our days off, we traveled all around the area having picnics, hiking, and just lying in the sun. The Great Smoky Mountains

National Park beckoned us time after time. We climbed the Chimney Tops (where the recent devastating fire started), hiked around Newfound Gap on the Tennessee-North Carolina state line, elevation 5,048 feet, and toured Cades Cove. One picnic I recall took place at the Chimneys Campground. We found numerous wooden tables scattered about and a few garbage cans attached to poles. We saw no other visitors that day, at least not at first, but as we sat eating our lunch a young black bear ventured nearby, checking the garbage cans. We sat quietly watching, and he soon wandered on, paying no attention to us. I remember another time driving out around the Farragut area west of Knoxville, a lot of which was undeveloped back then. We found a wide open field and spread out our towels. We lay there and soaked up the sun with my big portable radio (they were monsters at the time) providing background music.

My housing habits during this period were as unsettled as my family's back in my younger days. I roomed with the head of *The Journal*'s copy desk. I rented a room at the home of a fellow reporter, Ted York. And I rented a room from my former UT roomie, Bill Keel, who had married Jean Harmon, Alma's friend. During my days at the newspaper, I kept an eye on the teletype machine for developments in the Korean War. After the Chinese came down across the Yalu River, UN forces went into retreat all the way into South Korea. Seoul changed hands four times. The Defense Department began calling up reserve and National Guard units to bolster the troops we sent to Korea, and it didn't require a genius to divine the future of the 119th AC&W Squadron. One happy outcome for me was getting promoted to first lieutenant on May 17, 1951.

That summer I applied to attend the Air Intelligence

Chester D. Campbell

School at Lowry Air Force Base near Denver. They accepted me, and I received the required secret clearance. At the end of August, I said goodbye to Alma and set out across the country in my faithful Plymouth. I spent the first night around St. Louis, then headed west across the width of Missouri the next morning. There were no interstates, of course, and I had to slow down for every wide spot in the road, U.S. 40 to be precise. The weather looked fine during the day, some sun and a few clouds, but the clouds began to thicken by the time I reached Kansas City, which straddled the border with Kansas. I stopped on the far side of the city to eat supper and decided to push on a little farther before turning in. Darkness descended quickly with the cloud cover. Rain started to pepper down around an hour later, by the time I reached Topeka. I felt good, though, and kept going. Soon lightning flashes began to streak across the sky. After a healthy dose of that I decided I had better find shelter. The lightning intensified, striking all around the wide open Kansas plains. I stared into the darkness but saw no sign of a settlement large enough to provide accommodations. I thought about turning back, but a sign at a side road saved me, indicating the town of Manhattan lay eight miles to the north. I drove into the town, which did not appear all that big then, and found a sign marking an old hotel. The room looked as plain as an old hat, but the firm mattress provided a great night's sleep.

 The school at Lowry AFB started September 4 and lasted 60 days. I learned all about how the intelligence game worked. It primarily involved collection and analysis of information concerning enemy air operations, something I would find myself involved in soon. On weekends I toured the area, sometimes with other class members, most of the time alone. I've always been something of a loner. I visited Colorado Springs and marveled at the colorful sandstone spires at the Garden of the Gods. I wrote Alma regularly and talked to her on the phone a couple of times. We came up with a plan for Alma and Carrie to fly to Denver at the end of my school and drive back with me. When they arrived, I had a few days to spare before I needed to be back in Knoxville. We used them to see the area around Denver, including a trip up the Trail Ridge Road into the heights of the Rocky Mountains, 11,000 feet and above. We also visited an old Ghost Town with board sidewalks.

Not all, maybe, but most good things come to an end, and when the time came we packed the car to head back to Knoxville. We arrived just prior to the date when the 119th's activation orders took effect. On December 1, 1951, my unit became a part of the U.S. Air Force. I knew we wouldn't stay in Knoxville long, and in mid-January 1952, orders came transferring us to Otis Air Force Base on Cape Cod. Around this time, I learned later, my application for a top secret clearance had gone through the mill and FBI agents appeared in my Nashville neighborhood asking questions. These reports were not supposed to be seen by the individual concerned, but they came through my office and I read them. Not very exciting. And I received my clearance.

I had a dramatic introduction to the Northeast. I had heard the old saying: "It never snows on Cape Cod; when it snows in Boston, it rains on Cape Cod." My welcome snow must have measured a foot. Assigned to the Transient Officers Quarters, I woke up the next morning to a fire alarm going off along with overhead sprinklers. If you've never experienced a sprinkler in action, take my word, they put out a drenching rain. I heard somebody broke out a window and somehow set off the fire alarm.

Chester D. Campbell

I quickly got my permanent quarters and enjoyed a warm, dry room the next night. I found the Officers Club an interesting place at Otis. A lot of tall tales were spun there, but they weren't all tall. One of the regulars, Capt. Daniel "Chappie" James, Jr. of the 58th Fighter-Interceptor Squadron, had just returned from a tour of duty in Korea. He had flown 101 combat missions in P-51s and F-80s. He went on to become the first African-American four-star general in the Air Force. The 119th stayed at Otis until the end of the Korean War, but the base kept an air control and warning mission that changed with technical advances until its current description in the official website states: "Cape Cod Air Force Station is the only land based radar site providing missile warning for the eastern coast of the United States and southern Canada against intercontinental and sea-launched ballistic missiles."

My stay at Otis turned out to be rather brief. I arrived on January 24, and on April 3 I received orders from the 32nd Air Division transferring me to Camp Stoneman, California, for processing prior to departure for an assignment with Fifth Air Force in Korea. I didn't have to report to Camp Stoneman until April 28. I had enough leave to spend some time with Alma, and I did two things when I got back to Knoxville. First I traded in my old Plymouth Valiant for a new Dodge Coronet, then went to a jewelry store and bought an engagement ring. I gave Alma the ring and asked her to marry me. She said yes, but we agreed to wait until I got back from Korea. We drove to Nashville so she could meet my parents, then back to Knoxville. The last thing I did before I left was give her the keys to the new car. She didn't know how to drive, but her sister Bonnie's husband promised to teach her.

Everything But The Kitchen Sink

I arrived in San Francisco with a couple of days to spare before my reporting date at Camp Stoneman, located just to the east. Alma had a former student nurse friend from a large family in rural Sevier County–a place best known for Dolly Parton–who now lived in San Francisco. Gerry Garner had a little sister who later married Alma's brother Ira. When I looked her up on my arrival, Gerry proceeded to show me around the city. I remember roaming about The Presidio, the old fort that dated back to the time when Spain established it in 1776. It sat on the northwest corner of the city, just at the entrance to the Golden Gate Bridge, and not far to the west of Fort Mason, the port where I would depart for the Far East.

At Camp Stoneman, I went through the old military processing routine, checking all my records, getting my pay, and going through one routine I'll never forget. My arms were riddled with the pokes of hypodermic needles. I got at least five shots, probably more. They included ones to protect against the plague, typhus, yellow fever, and who knows what else. That night in the barracks I felt hot as a plate of Mexican tamales. I sweated until I fell into bed early. Surprisingly, I felt fine the next morning. And not long after I traveled to Fort Mason, where I boarded the USNS General W. F. Hase on May 8.

Manned by a civilian crew, the Hase had no separate dining facilities for officers. We ate with the crew, and we ate well. I probably gained several pounds during the voyage to Yokohama, Japan that lasted right at two weeks. We slept in bunks that were triple-deckers. I felt for the troops, who were packed down in the holds. The ship could carry 6,000 troops, but I don't think we had nearly that many. I never went down there, but I heard the smell from all the seasick guys really made it awful. Our route took us through both cold and warm climates. I spent most of my time on deck during the warm weather. I had brought along a small portable typewriter in a metal case, and I did a lot of writing along the way, including a rambling two-week long letter to Alma, which I still have. We did some kind of International Date Line crossing ceremony as is customary on naval vessels, but nothing significant enough to spark any particular memories. I do recall the lifeboat drills, when we had to don our life jackets and stand in front of the boats. For me the days passed without incident, and before long we debarked in Japan.

We were transported to another processing center. This one didn't use needles, and they weren't in a hurry. We had a few days to wander around the small town, which wasn't far from Tokyo. On May 26 I got orders transferring me to Headquarters Fifth Air Force, located in Seoul, South Korea. I received train tickets to Fukuoka on the southern island of Kyushu. The conductor shouted out the stops as we approached. I clearly remember the next to last one, when he shouted, "Hiroshima, Hiroshima." He pronounced it with the accent on the "o." At Fukuoka I boarded a C-54 for Korea.

I rode through the streets of Seoul, gawking at the results of fighting that had ended less than a year before. Along one stretch, only the train station appeared to be mostly intact. In another section of town, the Seoul National University campus appeared in good shape. Eighth Army had its headquarters on the main campus, while Fifth Air Force occupied the former medical school whose buildings were located on the other side of the street. When I arrived, I received a room assignment in a building used for officer housing, which included a barbershop with a Korean barber who displayed a permanent grin. The women who cleaned the rooms spoke bad English, but they knew how to place orders when one of us was heading to Japan.

A large three-story building housed the headquarters. I reported to the Intelligence Directorate on the second floor and was assigned to the Estimates Division. Our boss was a lieutenant colonel, with a captain as my immediate superior. He assigned me the primary job of monitoring enemy air activity. Intelligence officers in the flying units debriefed the aircrews after each mission and sent a report to us. I read them all and pulled out any mention of enemy activity. These came mainly from F-86 fighter-interceptor pilots, who reported on their tangles with Soviet-built MiG-15s, some piloted by North Koreans, others by Chinese or Russians. We also got reports from the F-84 fighter-bombers and F-94 nightfighters. I plotted these reports by date and location, which showed the MiGs coming in waves. They would appear just south of the Yalu River, North Korea's border with China, at first, then venture farther and farther south. It appeared the Communists were using the war as a training ground for pilots. They lost a lot of aircraft and pilots in the process. The Sabrejet pilots downed a total of 792 MiGs while losing only 76 F-86s by the end of the war. I lectured on the subject at United Nations air-ground school classes.

My badge permitted me entrance to just about any area of the complex. One off limits was the third floor of the headquarters building, location of an office vaguely called Supplemental Research. I was never told what they did, but from some information that came down, I guessed it involved radio intercepts and/or long range radar tracking, plus a little unconventional warfare.

When we weren't busy in the Estimates Division, sometimes I would head down the corridor to the Joint Operations Center where Air Force and other U.S. and allied service representatives directed air operations. I would then step into the adjoining room, the Tactical Air Control Center. There airmen wearing earphones used cue stick-like devices to move objects representing aircraft over a table-like representation of North Korea that covered most of the room. Friendlies were one color, enemy aircraft another. Controllers seated above could see the situation at a glance. There were sets of earphones around the room. I would pick up one and listen to the pilots talking to each other or to controllers. Another interesting experience I had a couple of times was crossing the street to Eighth Army Headquarters and attending the commander's briefing. It appeared a tightly scripted affair with staff officers stepping to the microphone to give reports. Lt. Gen. James Van Fleet occupied the commander's chair.

Although lowly lieutenants didn't merit their own vehicles at Fifth Air Force headquarters, I got an opportunity to see some of Seoul and parts of the Korean countryside in other ways. Doing a stint as Officer of the Day, I had a Jeep and a driver to shuttle me around to various installations that were part of the headquarters operation. About all I did amounted to confirmation that they were still there in one piece. I also traveled by Jeep to consult with intelligence officers at a couple of the air wings. I met with one at the 4th Fighter-Interceptor Wing at Kimpo Air Base, on the south side of the Han River from Seoul, also known as K-14. I also visited the 8th Fighter-Interceptor Wing at Suwon Air Base, which carried the designation of K-13. Kimpo, now called Gimpo, is an international airport serving Seoul, while

Suwon AB currently serves as a South Korean base. My recreational foray into the countryside came thanks to one of my old 119th AC&W buddies who had drawn an assignment as a transportation officer. He had his own Jeep. We wandered around an area with colorful temples and watched Korean girls frolic in their flowing *hanbok*, traditional Korean dresses.

With Buddhism the predominant religion in South Korea, I didn't have to go far to visit a Buddhist temple. But I don't think the Buddhists would have approved. Located near my living quarters, it bore the name The Temple Bar. Buddha was nowhere to be seen, but the colorfully painted structure had been turned into an officers club complete with bar, booze, and food. I visited it occasionally. By the end of July 1952 I qualified for an R&R (Rest and Recuperation) in Japan. My Korean cleaning lady ordered a pair of silk hose, for which she paid me in Korean won (we were required to use Military Payment Certificates, called MPCs). I caught a flight out of Kimpo to Tachikawa Air Base just outside Tokyo. I spent some time along the Ginza, a popular shopping area then but not as large and well-developed as today. I bought two large burgundy-colored cloisonné vases with ceramic flowers mounted on top, which I mailed to Alma. They sit on our current mantel in Nashville. R&Rs were short, and I soon returned to Seoul.

With the stalemate in the fighting along the 38th parallel, armistice talks dragged on at Panmunjom on the border between the two sides. We received transcripts of the daily discussions, and the diatribes by the North Korean participants were colorful if nothing else. They went on and on. One big sticking point involved our refusal to agree to return all communist prisoners. Many of them didn't want to go back to North Korea or China, fearing they would be shot. Ground fighting during that period amounted to small-scale actions that involved jockeying for positions around the mostly static battle line. Fifth Air Force continued to hammer away at targets inside North Korea and worked to keep any enemy air incursions from reaching the South, tasks that kept us busy in the Estimates Division. Besides putting out periodic estimates of the situation on the air war, we produced a daily intelligence summary called the DINTSUM for distribution to all flying units. That was one of my jobs.

In early November of 1952 I took another R&R in Japan. This time I stayed at the upscale Fujiya Hotel near Mt Fuji, a snow-capped volcano and the nation's highest mountain, about 80 miles from Tokyo. The scenic hotel featured traditional Japanese architecture with its tiled, hip-gabled roof, curved gables, and curved overhanging eaves. The restaurant menu featured American as well as Japanese dishes, and I ate heartily. As before, my R&R ended all too soon.

Back in Seoul, toward the middle of the month, I had the interesting experience of being named assistant defense counsel on a Special Courts-Martial. Apparently there were no real lawyers available as the major who served as defense counsel had no law degree either. A complete neophyte, I mostly watched and listened. In December I received an appointment as a member of another Courts-Martial. My main memory of that one dealt with a psychiatrist who testified for the defense. The way he sat and looked, and the way he talked, to me he appeared crazier than the defendant in the case. During that same month, I learned I had been promoted to captain. It was a spot promotion, a type of rank increase granted only in a combat zone. It would not last long in my case as my days in Korea were numbered. I received orders on March 26 transferring me to Higashi-Fuchu, Japan for return to the ZI (Zone of the Interior—military speak for the U.S.A.).

On April 3, just before leaving Korea, I was given a copy of orders awarding me the Bronze Star Medal. It stated the award was for meritorious service in connection with military operations against an enemy between May 30, 1952 and February 1,1953. The citation said "Campbell performed exceptionally meritorious service in support of operations in Korea as an Intelligence Officer in the Estimates Division, Directorate of Intelligence, Headquarters Fifth Air Force. He monitored enemy air activity over the Korean peninsula, contributed to daily intelligence summaries, and lectured on the subject at United Nations air-ground schools." I reverted to the rank of first lieutenant on April 10, the date I landed at Fuchu Air Force Base. I had a few days before I would be transported to Yokohama to board the U.S.S. General William Mitchell. I did a little shopping in Tokyo for trinkets to take home, but my biggest buy was a full eight-place setting of Noritake china at the base post exchange. It included all the little extras like cream pitcher, gravy bowl, and a large mixing bowl. They had the sets all packed and ready for shipping. I addressed it to Alma. We used them for many years until my last move when I gave them to grandson Andrew Campbell.

I boarded the General Mitchell on April 15, and the ship departed for Fort Mason, California. It was the ideal ship name for us Air Force types. General William "Billy"Mitchell is known as the father of the U.S. Air Force. After World War I, Mitchell, a vocal advocate of military aviation, received an appointment as assistant chief of the U.S. Army Air Service. Convinced that air power would be the most significant factor in future wars, he pushed for the creation of an independent air force. He even predicted a future war with Japan and said it would include an aerial attack on Pearl Harbor. His criticism of his superiors over aviation policy led to his Courts-Martial and retirement in 1926, the year after I came along.

The Mitchell provided a pleasant change from the USNS Hase that brought me to Japan. A larger and more commodious ship, the Mitchell was called a dependent ship because it carried families as well as troops. I still have the little fold-up brochure they gave us titled "Welcome Aboard," with a drawing of the Mitchell inside a ship's wheel. Unfolding it brought an outline of the full ship, showing all of it's facilities. Also included were such things as library hours, newspaper, entertainment, and religious services. I had a nicer cabin than on the Hase, and the large dining room proved quite pleasant. A couple of days out, we hit bad weather, creating rough seas, and the crowds at mealtime became slimmer. Having never been bothered by sea or air sickness, I ate heartily. The trip remained otherwise uneventful until we reached the Golden Gate, where we all cheered.

Back at Camp Stoneman, the endless processing continued. My orders from FEAF (Far East Air Forces) said I would be assigned to Parks AFB, California, and that's what my orders from Camp Stoneman dated April 27 confirmed. I don't recall what happened to change their mind—maybe someone remembered a message from Air Force Headquarters that said guys in my situation could get out if they wanted to—but I got orders the next day directing me to report to the commander at Warner Robbins Air Materiel Area, Warner Robbins, Georgia, for processing my release from active duty.

Meanwhile, I had other things on my mind. I flew to Knoxville for a reunion with Alma, who had learned to drive the Dodge. She quit her job at the hospital, we packed up the car and headed to my parents' home in Nashville. Her sister Carrie came with us. I quickly arranged things at the church where I grew up, we got a marriage license at the county court clerk's office, and on May 4, 1953, we were married. We drove south to Chattanooga and spent the first night on Lookout Mountain. We headed on down to Florida, where we spent just over a week walking on the beach and basking in the sun. Then it was up to Warner Robins, Georgia, home of Robins Air Force Base. I received my release from active duty on May 14. I got paid for 36 days accrued leave built up during my stay in Korea, and the commander, Major General K. E. Tibbetts, pinned the Bronze Star Medal on my uniform.

Chapter Five

NEWSPAPERS AND MAGAZINES

Back in civilian life, I pointed the nose of the Dodge toward Nashville and headed home with my new wife. I had a lot of money saved from my overseas tour since I found little to spend it on over there. We rented an apartment off Hillsboro Pike not far beyond Vanderbilt University. It occupied the front part of the second floor in a large three-story frame house. Our landlady was a tall, outspoken woman named Tillie, who had a young son. She also had a husband, but we saw little of him. The old fiction bug appeared again, and I decided to try my hand at writing short stories. I bought an old Underwood typewriter and a ream of paper and set to work. Alma also decided to go to work and got a job as a nurse in the obstetrics department at Mid-State Baptist Hospital (now St. Thomas Midtown). From the looks I got, Tillie didn't appreciate my staying home while Alma left for work in her crisp white uniform and cap.

To boost my chances, I signed up for a correspondence course from *Writer's Digest*. I picked a high goal for my magazine market choice, the magazine I had read as a teenager while sitting in the glider on the front porch: *The Saturday Evening Post*. I began to crank out short stories and send them to the *Post*. They kept coming back with small rejection slips attached. I finally began to get helpful rejection notes from a lady editor. Unfortunately, my efforts to find someone willing to buy my short stories, to put it succinctly, laid an egg. With Alma getting very pregnant, I turned to something I felt certain I could succeed at. In August of 1954 I went to work at *The Nashville Banner*, the city's evening newspaper. Like *The Knoxville Journal*, it had a conservative Republican bias in contrast to it's morning rival, the liberal *Nashville Tennessean*.

That same month I signed a contract with my buddy Dan Leech, who now worked as a contractor, to build us a house on a lot we bought in Madison, on the northeastern edge of Davidson County. The price of the house: $11,500. We paid $2,250 for the lot, a little less than an acre. In November, before Dan could finish the house, our first child arrived, a boy we named Stephen Douglas and called Steve. One quite interesting facet of this occurrence involved the doctor's bill. He didn't send one. Alma had worked at the hospital with one of Nashville's top obstetricians. He delivered all four of our children and never charged a penny.

I started out doing general assignments at the newspaper. At one point I became the city's first education reporter. I attended a six-week Education Reporting Seminar at Harvard University conduced by the Nieman Foundation for Journalism. In addition to gaining some valuable information, I enjoyed traveling around the greater Boston area, eating at some fine restaurants. I also basked in the warm weather, which proved much more hospitable than what I had experienced there in my early Air Force days.

When desegregation began in 1956, Clinton High School became the first Tennessee school affected. A photographer and I headed to East Tennessee when dynamite blasts rocked the building. Things remained tense while we were there, but no more violence. The governor had called out the National Guard to keep order. I don't remember anything too exciting, but I met one bigtime TV reporter from New York who acted like a know-it-all. During the 1957 session of the Tennessee General Assembly, I covered the House of Representatives. That was an educational experience, watching the devious things some of the legislators did. I thought one in particular should have been in prison. Toward the end of the legislative session, I took Alma to the hospital for the birth of our second son, Mark Alan. That fall I helped cover the Hattie Cotton school bombing in Nashville when the desegregation violence came home. Our kids weren't affected as no blacks lived in our area at the time.

During this same period I moved up a rank in the Air National Guard, gracing my uniform again with captain's bars. Taking advantage of my ANG status and my role as a newspaper reporter, I contacted the Second Air Force at Barksdale AFB near Shreveport, Louisiana and received permission to ride on a training flight in a B-47 Stratojet, then the Strategic Air Command's main nuclear-armed bomber. In turn, I would write a newspaper story about my experience. While there I heard sirens go off and learned it meant stay clear of particular streets as they transported atomic bombs from a heavily guarded area to the flight line. After my flight, I received a card appointing me an "Honorary SAC Crewmember." A little later, when they cleared the B-52 for news people, I got one of our Air Guard pilots to fly me in a T-33 jet trainer to Carswell AFB at Fort Worth, Texas. They suited me up and allowed me to attend the mission briefing. Out on the ramp, the monstrous B-52 looked bigger than ever. With its swept wings and eight jet engines, plus plenty of space for fuel storage, it had a range of more than 7,000 miles. We covered a lot of them that afternoon. I still have the Jet Navigation Charts showing the route we took, which the navigator gave me after the mission. We took off from Fort Worth and flew northwest to Amarillo, Texas, then took a more northerly course to Denver, Colorado. Heading west, we made our next turn at a checkpoint above the high mountains just north of Fillmore, Utah's first capital. From there we began our bomb run on Salt Lake City. The locations we "bombed" had facilities that scored the accuracy of our electronic bombing signal. We flew northwest to drop another load of "bombs" on Boise, Idaho, then followed that bomb run heading north to a turn near the Canadian border. After our next checkpoint to the south at Battle Mountain, Nevada, we turned southwest to Sacramento, California. From there we headed southeast to our final target, Los Angeles. After "bombs away" over LA, we turned due east and crossed half the country to Fort Worth. When we landed, I asked the pilot how much fuel we had left "Enough to get back to California," he said. Interestingly, these same B-52s, perhaps even the one I flew in 60 years ago, with modifications over the years, are still the backbone of America's airpower.

During my leisure time outside *Banner* hours, I began free-lancing non-fiction. One of the more intriguing incidents I came in contact with during my time as an intelligence officer in Korea involved a guy who wore faded olive drab fatigues with no insignia. I saw him one day hurrying through the corridor in the Fifth Air Force headquarters building with the head of Supplemental Research. I later learned that he commanded a group of South Korean irregulars who had set up a base on a small island off the western coast of North Korea. They were involved in intelligence collection. One clandestine operation took place deep inside North Korea in mid-April of 1951. Mike Roberts, not his real name but one I gave him in an article, and a team of four men flew in via an H-19 helicopter to bring out key parts and detailed photographs of a crashed MiG-15. A hair-raising tale that involved getting shot at by an enemy patrol on the ground and bracketed by antiaircraft fire on the way out, it gave us our first look at the Soviet's top fighter aircraft, a potential game changer that had suddenly appeared in the skies to challenge our air superiority. I wrote an article about the recovery operation that appeared in the November 1959 issue of *The American Legion Magazine*. I had read a brief account in a publication while at Fifth Air Force and knew it had been run by Col. Boyd Hubbard, Jr., Director of Intelligence at the time. I found him at Scott Air Force Base near St. Louis and interviewed him to get all the details. When I finished writing the article, I had to send it to the Air Force in Washington to get it cleared. After making several changes to satisfy the censors, I got an okay and soon sold it to the *Legion Magazine*.

Along the way, the powers that be at the newspaper discovered that I knew how to spell and had a good grasp of English grammar. For my last year at *The Banner* they put me on the copy desk, where stories approved by the city editor went for final editing and headlines written. I preferred writing but determined to make the best of it. I did my share of writing at home, of course. During lulls on the copy desk, I would take out a sheet of paper and type out ideas to follow up at home. One of my superiors, I think he carried the title of managing editor, took exception to this and one day said, "If you like doing this so much, you can just do it at home." With that, he had me fired. This news didn't strike me as something Alma would be happy to hear since she had just given birth to our first daughter, Sarah Anne, a few weeks before. We named her after Alma's mother but called her Anne.

In December of 1959, I did indeed go home to freelance magazine articles. I built a small, make that tiny, office in one corner of the garage and went to work. I sold articles to publications such as *Coronet*, *Air Progress*, and *The Rotarian*. Working in the garage gave me a little more access to Alma and the kids, but this would be my last opportunity to enjoy that kind of homey atmosphere for a long time. After nine months I got a call from my former *Banner* editor saying James Metcalfe had an opening for an account executive at Metcalfe Public Relations Agency, and he had recommended me. I took the job and became primarily responsible for handling public relations activities for the City of Nashville. While working with Mayor Ben West and his staff, I generated lots of ideas. For one I wrote scripts and supervised production of a series of TV specials that appeared on the local public television channel. They told the stories of Nashville area landmarks that included The Hermitage, home of President Andrew Jackson, and Travellers Rest, the home built in 1799 by John Overton, one of the first justices of the Tennessee Supreme Court. He also happened to be a friend and advisor to Andrew Jackson. In addition, I wrote news releases on various city activities.

June of 1961 brought us to the delivery room at Baptist Hospital for the last time. We welcomed our second daughter, Carrie Elizabeth, who became Betsy. Then came another major shift in my life. In the summer of 1962, Jim Metcalfe's son came into the business. With little forewarning, Jim told me he couldn't afford two account executives, that I'd have to go. One person in the office, the only other one, in fact, thought I got a bum deal—Mikie Evans, Metcalfe's secretary. More of her shortly.

A former *Nashville Banner* staffer and friend from East High days bailed me out. Eddie Jones, who graduated in the same class as brother Jim, had been picked to serve as executive vice president of the Nashville Area Chamber of Commerce. He recommended me for his old job, writing speeches for Governor Buford Ellington. I knew I would not be there long, since the governor's term ended in January. My time with the State of Tennessee illustrated how political organizations work. My instructions specified that I could do anything I wanted with my time as long as I got my speeches written. I occupied a position in the Department of Revenue, but I only picked up my checks there. With all that free time I put together a plan for something I had been wanting to do, publish a local magazine. Locating a copy of *Atlanta Magazine*, I studied it thoroughly, then made a trip to Atlanta to talk with the editor. The chamber of commerce owned Atlanta's magazine, but the Nashville chamber had neither the budget nor the will to take on such a project. I approached several potential investors I knew, including Tom Cummings, a fellow officer in the Air Guard, whose sign company now operated all over the country. He didn't want to get involved in a business he knew nothing about. A businessman friend helped me look, but the idea was too different for Nashville. Nobody thought it would fly here. I did, and I doggedly plowed ahead.

I had struck up an acquaintance with three guys who ran Illustration-Design/Group (IDG), a commercial art studio, and asked if they knew of anybody who might be interested in being the magazine's art director. They suggested I contact an artist who worked for the

Methodist Publishing House. When I cornered Hermann Zimmermann and laid out what I had in mind, he smiled, which was about the most you could expect from the taciturn German immigrant, and he agreed to join me. I had already approached Mikie Evans, Jim Metcalfe's secretary, and she agreed to serve as business and circulation manager. The three of us came up with around $1,500 for starting capital.

The next task proved a major hurdle. I knew that advertising played a crucial role in a magazine's success. I'm a low-key guy who never liked pushing myself on other people, but I had made a good start in that direction during my attempt to locate a financial backer. Having no alternative, I became the de facto advertising salesman. Happily, most of the people I called on liked the idea of a magazine for Nashville. I just had to convince them that it could succeed. The ads would not be billed, of course, until the publication came out. Hermann provided me with some good promotional artwork, including brochures promoting subscriptions, and I concentrated mostly on advertising agencies. Some of them agreed to contact their clients. I buttonholed friends at *The Banner* for articles, pointing out that I could offer little if any compensation. I think they were lured by the prospect of seeing their by-lines in a slick-paper magazine. Their names helped out with the advertisers, particularly that of *Banner* sports editor Fred Russell, who was quite popular and well known, having written articles for *The Saturday Evening Post*, that elusive publication I had chased with my short stories. *Banner* staffers wrote every article in the first issue except for those I created and one by an ad agency buddy. Dave Baker, one of the IDG partners, provided the front cover, a stylized, full-color painting of downtown Nashville from an aerial viewpoint. Doyne Advertising Agency ran a full-color ad on the back cover. The owners of a luxury high-rise apartment building plus the electric and gas companies were the only other full-page advertisers. I sold a total of seven and three-fourths pages of advertising, which amounted to 18 percent of the 44-page issue, hardly enough to pay the printer's and engraver's bills, let alone anything for the staff and writers. The printer of the first issue demanded payment before he would print the second one. That resulted in a switch to another printer. The first guy later agreed to take out some of his delinquent bill in advertising. The new printer also ran regular ads.

The operation did not just run on a shoestring, more like a thread, but it was a shiny thread. The Premier Issue hit the newsstands on January 10, 1963 and promptly sold out. It received an Award of Merit from the Mead Corporation, a paper manufacturer. Besides all the work I did on the issue, I spent as much time as I could on promoting my creation. I picked up the first copy from the printer on January 8 and showed it to Nashville on WSM-TV's "Noon" show. I discussed it with two radio personalities the following day, and did the same the next day on a popular morning radio show. I also had to get out and sell advertising for the second issue. One article scheduled for February featured skiing on the slopes in Gatlinburg. I drove up there and spent a few days calling on hotels, restaurants, any kind of business that appeared a possible advertiser. I totally struck out. I intended to get the publication in the mail
to subscribers before the end of the month prior to the date on the cover, but production problems delayed the January issue. Problems continued to spiral out and it became obvious we would be even later with the next

a few days calling on hotels, restaurants, any kind of business that appeared a possible advertiser. I totally struck out. I intended to get the publication in the mail to subscribers before the end of the month prior to the date on the cover, but production problems delayed the January issue. Problems continued to spiral out and it became obvious we would be even later with the next issue, so I decided to call it February-March and get it out the middle of February. In a note on the contents page, I promised future editions would appear on time. One possibility I didn't count on, I ran into trouble with the Post Office. Our second class (cheap rate) mail permit called for a monthly publication, not bimonthly. I made Impassioned promises that I would never ever put out a two-month issue again, and they let us keep our permit.

I continued to spend one weekend a month at Berry Field, the Nashville airport, training with the 118th Air Transport Wing of the Tennessee Air National Guard. I served as the wing intelligence officer and received a promotion to major. Prior to being bumped up to group and then wing level, I had been assigned to the 105th Air Transport Squadron, a lineal descendant of the 105th Observation Squadron that I had visited as a youngster.

By the third issue of *Nashville Magazine*, in April, I had begun working several issues ahead. And during April I hired an advertising manager, which freed me to concentrate on the editorial content. I had been working fourteen and sixteen hours a day, leaving little time for home and family. It wouldn't get much better during the next few years, which was tough on my wife and four kids. The magazine jumped to 52 pages in May, and advertising improved, though still not enough.

Letters to the editor raved about the quality of the content and appearance of the magazine. We published laudatory letters from business leaders and educators, including the new chancellor of Vanderbilt University.

including the new chancellor of Vanderbilt University. The first year ended with Hermann Zimmermann, the hard-nosed German with a thick accent who had helped launch the project, deciding he'd sacrificed enough. It would take several years before we came up with another art director to equal his talent.

    A young artist named Tom Seigenthaler, younger brother of the morning newspaper's editor, stepped in as art director. He stayed with us for four issues. Several years later, Tom started Seigenthaler Public Relations, which developed into what is now one of the largest PR firms in the South. When Tom left, I faced another of the many black holes that marked my career as editor. I had no luck finding a new art director, and the next issue was ready to go, except for being laid out for the printer. I figured I had learned enough from Hermann to get it done. So I did. I included no art director in the staff listings, and where I usually ran a description of the cover, it said simply "Design by C. C. Douglass, photos by Joe Bomar/Joe Thain." The C. C. stood for Chester Campbell; Douglas was my middle name, though I used the double "s" as my ancestors did. The issue certainly won no awards for its design, but it kept things alive until I could get a new art director, which I did for the next issue.

    Tupper Saussy, the creative genius behind the McDonald and Associates advertising agency (later McDonald and Saussy), had been intrigued by the magazine and offered to serve as art director, no charge. It was an offer I couldn't refuse. I had sized the magazine on a typical 8½ by 11 format, but after a few months Tupper talked me into increasing the size to 9 by 12. We kept the unwieldy format for a couple of years. Tupper came up with some wild ideas that kept things interesting. He went on to pursue his interest in music, best known as the songwriter and keyboardist for the psychedelic pop band The Neon Philharmonic. Their rendition of his song "Morning Girl" made it to the Top Twenty and was nominated for two Grammies in 1969, three years after he quit working on *Nashville Magazine.*

We had some excellent writers in addition to those I recruited from the ranks. The third issue featured our first fiction, a short story, *The Whippoorwill Is a Southern Bird,* a Civil War tale by Alfred Leland Crabb, professor of education at Peabody College (now part of Vanderbilt University) and author of several historical novels. I don't remember what we paid him, but it wasn't much. Dr. Crabb authored a two-part article titled "City of Books " during the second year of publication. Another local author who wrote for us, Jesse Hill Ford, gained fame in 1964 for a teleplay and theatrical script titled "The Conversion of Buster Drumwright."

Despite the burden of finding writers for articles and photographers to illustrate them, editing the finished products (and many of them required heavy editing), plus writing my own articles and features like "Scene About Town" at the front and "Loose Ends" on the back page, the job had its enjoyable part. I was invited to numerous parties and functions, I interviewed many important personalities, and I covered events such as President Lyndon Johnson speaking at the opening of Percy Priest Dam on the east side of Nashville. All the bigwigs around town knew me, and most thought I was providing a valuable service, though I'm sure some of them questioned my sanity for doing it.

As I mentioned earlier, my long hours at work left little time for home and family, but I did manage to squeeze in some junkets now and then. We made visits to Alma's younger brother in Clearwater, Florida, who to Alma's younger brother in Clearwater, Florida, who had two kids with ages similar to ours. And we took several trips to Knoxville, where her two sisters lived. I remember one around this time when I decided to take Steve and Mark on a hiking trip to Mt. LeConte in the Great Smoky Mountains National Park. Anne begged to go with us, but I thought the climb would be too much for her since she hadn't reached her tenth birthday yet. LeConte, the highest peak in the Smokies, reached an elevation of 6593 feet. When we got ready to leave, she wouldn't come out of the house. After we got home she wouldn't talk to me. She became a rugged outdoor type later, and I realized she likely would have made the hike okay. It took her a long time to forgive me for that one.

When Tupper Saussy moved on, a young woman named Cia Houston took over as art director of *Nashville Magazine* in June of 1966. After a few issues, she scrapped the arty logo Tupper had created for the cover and returned to a simpler "Nashville" heading reminiscent of Hermann Zimmermann's original design. Cia stayed for seven issues, then Walt Thomas came on board with the January 1967 issue. By that time things were not going well at all. We had cut back to 36-page issues, and advertisers were hardly flocking to our pages. I came up with an idea to promote subscriptions, more readers being the key to more ads, which we featured in full page promos. We put together a number of prizes, thanks to the companies that provided them for only a mention in the magazine, which people could win with a coupon used for low-rate lifetime subscriptions. The grand prize was an all-expense-paid week for two at the San Antonio World's Fair. Meanwhile, an article in the March issue won us another award. To quote from the morning newspaper:

Everything But The Kitchen Sink

"'Death of a Police Career,' an article which appeared in the March 1967 issue of *Nashville Magazine*, has been named the best urban affairs article for that year for city periodicals."

The Metropolitan Magazine Association composed of 22 city magazines around the country, nearly all representing city's larger than Nashville, presented the award. The article told of problems encountered by retired Lt. R. B. Owen while serving with the Nashville and Metro police departments. His main concern was the influence of politicians on the department. He said officers were promoted when they were unqualified or even ineligible for the position.

I enjoyed getting awards, but they didn't help our situation. I had talked a few friends into investing a little money in the magazine, and they were getting antsy. I also had a $3,000 90-day note (a fair sum in those days) I had renewed over and over, thanks to a friendly vice president at Third National Bank. Dr. Norman Cassell, the pediatrician who looked after all four of our kids, co-signed the note and stuck with me patiently. Mikie Evans, the other original staff member, had left because of the shortage of funds to pay salaries. I knew I had to come up with a solution fast because most everyone else had lost their patience. Walter Barrett, head of advertising and public relations for Life & Casualty Insurance Company, one of the city's top firms, had been a trusted friend and advisor. He also placed L&C ads in the magazine. Guilford Dudley, Jr., a prominent Nashvillian who served as Ambassador to Denmark under Presidents Nixon and Ford, headed L&C at the time. I prevailed on Barrett to try and convince Dudley, a civic-minded leader, to arrange for Life & Casualty to buy the magazine. He succeeded. I got enough to pay off the note, plus the

the note, plus the printer, engraver, and typographer, with a small amount left for the stockholders. This period brought another change in my life. After serving in the Tennessee Air National Guard since my release from active duty in the Korean War, I was promoted to lieutenant colonel but no vacancies existed for an officer of that rank. As a result, I was forced out of the Guard and into the Air Force Reserve. With no reserve outfit to join, they relegated me to inactive status.

Meanwhile, *Nashville Magazine* moved from small quarters on Union Street to the twenty-first floor of the L&C Tower, then the tallest building in town. The May 1968 issue came out on time and sported a bold new masthead, a new art director, Kenneth Thompson, and at the top of the staff listing: Nashville Magazine, Inc., Guilford Dudley Jr., President. I changed my back page feature from "Loose Ends" to "Last Word." In it I wrote the "new logotype, designed by our new art director, Ken Thompson, lends a uniqueness and originality that I feel is characteristic both of the magazine and of the city whose name it bears." I loved the swirling artwork but, unfortunately, it turned out to be too close to somebody else's logo for the L&C lawyers. Ken had to redesign it for the next issue. I also quoted from Dudley's comments in the L&C news release, written by Walt Barrett,
I'm sure: *Nashville Magazine* "has long been recognized for its quality and we hope to expand its influence and acceptance in the community." One other small point I should mention here. From the first issue we used Data Service Corp. with its new IBM 1401 computer to maintain our mailing list and produce mailing labels. When we got boxes of magazines from the printer, we had to stick the labels on and bundle the magazines according to Post Office regulations. We sent new address

Everything But The Kitchen Sink

lists to Data Service each month to be put on punch cards and fed to the computer. Keeping up with all this came under the heading of "circulation." Early on I listed the circulation assistant as Maude Campbell, my Mom, who helped with the paper work. In the staff listings for the new L&C magazine I put her up there in large type as Circulation Manager.

Everything went fine at first. We soon beefed up the staff, including a fulltime circulation manager to replace Mom, and increased the size of the issues. But after a few months the staff listing included a new member identified as "Gen. Mgr. & Executive V. President." I learned from Walt Barrett that he had been brought in by the L&C vice president as a favor to a close friend. He was a recovering alcoholic. I didn't care for the way he handled things, believing he hadn't recovered sufficiently, but I decided I would keep hands off as long as he didn't try to interfere with the editorial content.

About this time I wrote one of my most interesting articles, which we highlighted on the cover with a photo of the M/V John S. Herbert, home port Nashville, Tennessee. The opening page of the article featured another of our new features, editorial color. The photo taken from the front of a sand-filled barge showed the pilot house of the "John S.," as she was known along the waterways, in the background cruising along the Cumberland River. I had two photographers with me, Ken Thompson shooting black and white and another one shooting color. We met the towboat a little after eleven a.m. near Dover, Tennessee, 83 miles northwest of Nashville. The captain angled his 435-foot tow beside the bank for uscolor. The photo taken from the front of a sand-filled barge showed the pilot house of the "John S.," as she was known along the waterways, in the background

background cruising along the Cumberland River. I had two photographers with me, Ken Thompson shooting black and white and another one shooting color. We met the towboat a little after eleven a.m. near Dover, Tennessee, 83 miles northwest of Nashville. The captain angled his 435-foot tow beside the bank for us to board. Although they called the John S. a towboat, it actually pushed the barges, in this case eight of them filled with 3600 tons of sand and gravel for Herbert Materials in downtown Nashville. The largest of Herbert's fleet of boats, the John S. had been built three years previously by Nashville Bridge Company. It boasted all the comforts of home, including a well appointed galley that served copious quantities of great food.

 The boat and its lengthy cargo plodded along at eight miles an hour. We had to slow when passing a group of TVA barges docked at the site of what would become the Cumberland City Steam Plant. And we had to stop to navigate the lock at Cheatham Dam. It resulted in a journey that would last until one a.m. It turned out to be the most leisurely voyage I've ever taken. At that speed you have time to take note of every little detail, every change in the scenery about you. It inspired me to open my article with a sensuous and somewhat flowery description of what it looked and felt like when evening arrived.

 "The sunset comes slowly, painting the clouds in broad, shifting strokes of yellow, then red deepening to purple, and finally an inky blue that slips quietly into black. It makes a striking sight anywhere, but on the river it seems to take on a special quality. The water, a deep green in the sunlight, except where the huge blades beneath the boat churn it into a frothy white wake, gradually blackens as the trees and bluffs along the riverbanks merge into dark silhouettes. The heat of the summer day fades with the darkness, and on the ladder outside the pilot house, high above the water that shimmers yellow beneath the running lights, a cool breeze piques the nostrils with a characteristic river smell and sends chill bumps rippling over bare arms."

We published some good issues that fall, and I enjoyed working with Ken, but by the end of 1968 my patience had worn thin with the exec v.p. Walt and I couldn't prevail on Guilford Dudley to do anything about it. I talked with an old friend I had worked with at the newspaper who now ran Noble-Dury & Associates, the city's largest advertising and public relations agency. He offered me a job, and on February 6 I submitted my resignation as editor of *Nashville Magazine*. I hated to give up on the project I had devoted so much time and effort to, but I could see it headed in the wrong direction. Although my name did not appear in the staff listing of the March issue, they let me write my Last Word column on the back page. I started by writing that it could more aptly be titled *The Very Last Word*. I reflected on some of my hopes for the magazine and concluded with this paragraph:

"*Nashville Magazine* came into being about the same time as Metropolitan Nashville, and we have both suffered from our growing pains. But an editor could not have asked for a more significant or more eventful era in which to ply his trade. It has been fun; it has been heartbreaking. It has brought the heights of fulfillment and the depths of despair. But mostly it has led to a profound respect for the heavy responsibility to the public that rests on one who dares to place himself into such a position. I can only hope that in your eyes I proved worthy of the job."

The ad salesman who had been with me before L&C

Chester D. Campbell

took over left at the same time I did. About three months later, Ken Thompson decided he'd had enough and hung up his artist portfolio. They didn't hire a replacement art director, and you could tell it. The layouts looked less professional, and the eye-pleasing white space disappeared. By late fall, advertising dropped and the issues had been cut back to 36 pages. Shortly after the first of 1970, the magazine I had labored over with such high hopes ceased publication.

Chapter Six

ADVERTISING AND PUBLIC RELATIONS INTERLUDE

THE NEWS RELEASE from Noble-Dury & Associates announcing my departure from *Nashville Magazine* and my decision to join the advertising agency quoted a letter to the magazine from D. R. Buttrey, past president, and Edward F. Jones, executive vice president, of the Nashville Area Chamber of Commerce. Referring to me, the letter said:

"We think the entire community is in your personal debt for six years of touch-and-go service to Nashville. The January issue begins the seventh year of what was for a long time a determined one-man effort."

In the spring of 1969, I joined Noble-Dury's Creative Department as an advertising copy writer. I created newspaper ads and radio and TV commercials for a variety of clients. Familiar names included Kentucky Fried Chicken and Martha White Flour. As for the latter, I wrote commercials for the Flatt and Scruggs Show and listened to them live when I attended tapings with the account executive who handled Martha White. The most fun I had on this job took place when we got a funeral home and cemetery owner as a client. He wanted us to promote a new concept he had for a high-rise mausoleum. It struck me as a weird and funny idea. I've always had a bent for the satirical, and this looked made-to-order. I wrote a straight advertisement, then I dummied up a full page with parodies of the high-rise burial place. It got lots of laughs around the office, but I tore it up in case the client should happen by and spot it.

My move to Noble-Dury was not the only big change that year. With our older son Steve nearly fifteen and Mark not far behind, we needed a larger bedroom and another bath. I found a contractor and showed him how I wanted the addition to use the attached single car garage entered from the kitchen door. It would provide room for a bath (my old office) and a den, plus an extension for a bedroom. I also wanted an attached two-car garage. They completed the job in late fall. The boys loved their new "private" digs, and the rest of us were equally happy with less traffic in our bathroom.

When Jim Elliott decided to beef up the public relations side of Noble-Dury, called NDPR, he asked me to move over and join the guy who was running it. I wrote news releases and visited a client in Alabama to work on plans for a PR campaign. Things bounced along smoothly for a few months, and then I did something I likely should have approached in a slightly different way. As Yogi Berra would have said, "It's deja vu all over again." In October 1970 an old friend from my days in the Society of Professional Journalists, known then as Sigma Delta Chi, handled a magazine for the Tennessee Association of Life Underwriters (TALU). He had taken a job in Washington and asked if I'd be interested in putting out the quarterly publication. That was like asking an old race horse would you like to run? I said sure. I never thought of it being something NDPR would be interested in. Wrong. When Elliott heard about it a few months later, he said I should have acquired the the TALU magazine and maybe some others for the agency. They decided NDPR no longer needed a second account executive. Exit Campbell, again.

I did another exit in 1970. After being assigned to the Air Force Reserve on departing from the Tennessee Air National Guard, I did a couple of correspondence courses to stay active, but Noble-Dury kept me busy and I let things slip with the AF Reserve. Late in 1970 I received a letter saying I had two choices: I could resign my commission or retire. I obviously chose the latter, becoming Lt. Col. Chester D. Campbell, USAFR Retired. The retired pay wouldn't come along until I reached 65, and it hasn't been all that great, though handy to have and a help at keeping us solvent. The great part turned out to be Tricare for Life, medical insurance that pays the Medicare deductible plus whatever Medicare doesn't pay.

Chapter Seven

FINDING MY GROOVE

LET'S SEE HOW MANY jobs I had held up to this point, around my forty-fifth birthday. Starting from the beginning, I workecd as a drugstore cowboy, electrician's helper, sold women's shoes, order filler at Washington Manufacturing Company, mail sorter at the Post Office, aviation cadet in the Army Air Forces, freelance writer, newspaper reporter, Air Force intelligence officer, newspaper copy editor, public relations account executive, speech writer for a governor, magazine editor and publisher, and advertising copy writer. That's fourteen jobs. Some people, like my brother Jim, worked their entire lives at one job. Look what they missed. But now I stood at the brink of number fifteen, my longest and next to the last job.

The Tennessee Association of Life Underwriters' affairs had been managed by a retired secretary, and she wanted to retire again. They offered me that part-time job in addition to the magazine, which was called *Tennessee Life Insurance News*. As with anything new I approached, I did a quick study and learned a bit about the field of association management. I decided to set up a multiple management firm, working out of my home, and looked around for other clients. I produced magazines for restaurant associations of Tennessee, Georgia, and Alabama; the Tennessee Nurses Association, and the Tennessee Association of Realtors.

Additionally I managed the Tennessee Restaurant Association for a while. Early in the game I took some courses in photography and cinematography at Nashville State Technical Institute, gaining information helpful on the job. I joined the American Society of Association Executives (ASAE) and began getting its excellent magazine. That led me to attend the ASAE annual convention where I picked up lots of valuable ideas. I made enough off the multiple management firm to live on while impressing the Life Underwriters' leadership with my management skills. TALU's members were life insurance agents, general agents and managers. Some were top agents whose commissions made them quite well off. One who took over as TALU president in the summer of 1973 believed in thinking big. He wanted me to drop my other commitments and accept management of only Life Underwriters. In preparation for it, he arranged in the budget for me to receive an attractive salary.

On July 1, 1973 I became the fulltime executive vice president of TALU, opened an office, and hired a secretary. I changed *Tennessee Life Insurance News* to bimonthly and began tackling membership. The association had grown by only 326 members between 1965 and 1970, but programs I developed helped boost membership from 3,326 in 1970 to 4,413 by 1975. That August I received the CAE (Certified Association Executive) designation from ASAE after a comprehensive daylong examination in Montgomery, Alabama. Later I completed nine courses to earn ASAE's Certificate in Convention Management. I think the phase of association management I enjoyed most was putting on the annual TALU convention. I let my imagination run wild, expanded the program to three days, and originated sophisticated productions with special audio-visual presentations. We rotated the convention around the state, and when it came Nashville's turn I used local TV personalities in the productions. As another facet of convention management, I created distinctive themes each year. I also sold exhibit space, growing it over time to more than 30 booths, which brought in more funds to finance the programs. I continued to gain ideas from attendance at the annual ASAE Conventions, which took place in major cities around the continental U.S., plus Honolulu, Toronto, and Acapulco, Mexico. I took Alma with me on many of those trips.

Using skills I had acquired earlier, I handled complete production (writing, photography, sound recording) for a 13½-minute tape narrated color slide presentation titled "Insuring Your Future," aimed at explaining life insurance to high school students. We made copies available to local associations across the state, of which there were some twenty plus. Although I initiated, completed, or materially assisted in a wide variety of programs and activities of the association, the ordinary member, as well as many board members, would not have been aware of my role in them. My personal management style called for me to work in the background and give the volunteers credit for as much as possible.

Managing the association kept me busy, but in 1973 the old fiction bug sneaked out again. In my free time I wrote another novel. Titled *The Music Played Red*, it traded on my love of the spy genre. The book involved Russians, a defecting Bulgarian physicist who became a Vanderbilt professor, and involvement with the music business. I sent it to several publishers, and it stuck for awhile with Avon Books in New York. After nearly six months I got the manuscript back with a letter from Avon's executive editor. He wrote, "There were several favorable readings, but they were not strong enough to overcome our bias against suspense fiction." With the press of TALU business, I put *The Music Played Red* aside.

In addition to TALU, I served as executive director and treasurer of the Life Underwriters Political Action Committee. In 1974 we started an annual Legislative Dinner for the legislative leadership and members of the Commerce Committees of the two houses of the state legislature. It allowed us to get acquainted with the legislators so they would know who we were if we approached them with a problem. For several years the association president and I paid get-acquainted visits to the governor. I have a stack of photos made with various governors, including one who served a prison term for crimes he committed while in office. Another photo is with Gov. Lamar Alexander, now U.S. Senator Alexander who is chairman of the powerful Senate Health, Education, Labor, and Pensions Committee.

I felt a heavy burden for not having spent more time with my children when they were growing up. Years went by when I barely saw them. They'd be in bed when I got home, and I hardly had time for saying more than good-bye when they left for school. Things got a little better after I settled down with TALU. I took vacations and we visited Alma's younger brother in Clearwater, Florida several times. My older son, Steve, wasn't much on the athletics side, but the younger one, Mark, played football in high school, and we went to all his games. Anne, my older daughter, was athletic and played basketball. She also liked tennis, and during the mid 1970s we played together a lot. We established a rapport that has continued to this day. As the only unmarried child, she has the freedom to come to Nashville and visit more often.

As the association grew during this period, the tasks required of the staff grew as well. We added another female member and moved into larger quarters in the suburban Tennessee Hospital Association Building. We used the THA board room for our board meetings, and overall it made for a much more upscale operation. TALU probably ranked as the largest association in the state member-wise, though hardly the wealthiest. But my salary increased each year and I got a leased car to use, since my job required me to visit as many of the local associations as possible. I usually made talks at their meetings and became a seasoned speaker, if not a terribly polished one. I made lots of good friends, particularly among the state presidents, who served only one year. They included an old UT journalism friend who had gone into the life insurance business instead of plying his trade as a scribe.

I took an active role as well in the organization for association executives of state groups affiliated with the National Association of Life Underwriters headquartered in Washington, D.C. I served on the Association Executives Advisory Council and helped plan agendas for the annual meeting. We always arrived at the NALU Convention site a few days early to hold our sessions. I'll never forget one year when we met at the Shoreham Hotel in Washington. I arrived before my TALU members and took part in the association execs activities. Like most of the other states, we always had a Tennessee Suite where we entertained visitors with good ol' Southern hospitality and good ol' Tennessee whiskey. Jack Daniel always gave us a case of Old No. 7 which I brought in the trunk of my car. When I stopped by my room intending to check on the suite, I left the door open, prepared to go right back out. I heard a noise and turned to face a man holding a pistol pointed at me, his face masked with a kerchief. He ordered me to hand over my money. I don't remember how much I had in my billfold, but it was less than $100. Then he told me to take off my belt and turn around. He bound my hands with it and told me not to leave the room for fifteen minutes. I was pretty well shaken, but as soon as I gathered my wits I called the hotel and reported what had happened. I doubted he would be waiting for me, but I took my time opening the door.

I became quite the celebrity when my TALU members began arriving. The hotel was surrounded by cops as a motorcycle assembly happened to be in the area. A little later a pair of D.C. detectives questioned me about the guy. Because of the mask, I couldn't have identified him if they'd showed me a photo. They said they were fairly sure of his identity. As soon as he left my room, he had gone up one floor and robbed a couple checking into their room. I didn't hear any more of it, but the hotel reimbursed the money I lost. The convention went on unhindered. The only other thing I recall from that event involved one evening when the Alaska delegation sponsored a cookout featuring salmon they had flown in. Tasty.

My most memorable national convention took place in 1980 in Hawaii. Alma accompanied me to that one, and at the closing ceremony of the execs meeting, they presented me the C. Carney Smith Award "for the advancement of professionalism in association management." The award is still given by NAIFA (National Association of Insurance and Financial Advisors), the name that succeeded NALU. Carney Smith managed the association for many years, including the time of my affiliation with the organization. The year 1980 also marked another milestone in my association management career. I had been a member of the Tennessee Society of Association Executives since early in my time as an association exec. After "going through the chairs" from secretary to treasurer to vice president, this was the year that I became president. I don't remember any great accomplishments that occurred during my administration, but I recall the officers and committee chairmen enjoyed a planning retreat I set up near the beach in Florida.

An occurrence in 1980 brought *The Music Played Red* back to life. While digging through a large drawer in my desk, I came across a box with the manuscript inside. I pulled it out and decided it needed a major overhaul. After the revision, and a couple of name changes, I submitted *Operation Boomerang* to a few agents. One returned the manuscript with a brief note saying their readers had some nice things to say though not enough for an acceptance. I wrote and asked for the full reports from the readers. She complied, and they had some excellent points. In addition to problems the readers mentioned, the agent said the market for this kind of story had become quite poor. She thought I should turn to something else. The *Boomerang* made a circular orbit and soared back into its box.

TALU continued to grow and gain national recognition. We put members on the national board and had others who played major roles in the industry. I kept up my annual jaunt to the ASAE conventions but had a sad ending to the one in 1982. I left early because of a call from home advising that my mother suffered from a serious illness. I arrived in time to see her, but she died a few days later at age 82. She had been a stabilizing force in my life when I needed her, and I felt her loss deeply.

Two years later, Alma and I joined a couple from our Sunday School class, Betty and Jim McClellan, in signing up for a European tour run by a travel agent friend of theirs. We landed at Schiphol Airport in Amsterdam to begin our tour. One of the first things we did took us on a boat through the canals. We saw the house where Anne Frank lived and wrote her famous diaries while in hiding. The next day we boarded a bus that would be our headquarters for the rest of our journey through Europe, which led us first into Germany. After a visit to Cologne, with its striking twin-towered cathedral that remained intact after World War II, despite bombing that flattened the city, we headed down the Rhine valley. Somewhere along the way, probably around Koblenz, we embarked on a Rhine riverboat for a southbound cruise. They pointed out significant spots we passed, including the Lorelie Rock, a stone promontory with a legend behind it. According to the story, a nymph named Lorelie lived atop the rock and sang such an alluring song sailors passing by couldn't resist it and crashed their boats against the rock. Our captain obviously didn't succumb to the siren song and we disembarked at the next port of call. When we made it to Munich, Germany's third largest city, we visited the former concentration camp at nearby Dachau. A dark, blustery day, it seemed fitting for what we experienced. We saw the gas chambers and watched a movie that showed Jews being brought in on trains. From there we traveled southwest to the small town of Oberammergau, where the local people put on their famed Passion Play. Normally they produced it every tenth year that ended with a zero, but 1984 marked the 350th anniversary of its beginning. People from all over the world came to see the show.

Chester D. Campbell

    The next leg of our tour took us through the Bavarian Alps, passing near Hitler's "Eagles Nest" hideaway at Berchtesgaden. Then we traveled through the Brenner Pass into Austria, through Innsbruck, down to Italy, where we stopped at Venice. Cruising through the canals in a gondola made for a leisurely but exciting morning. We got off at Piazza San Marco (St. Mark's Square) and wandered about the small alleyways and their variety of shops. We had no problem getting around, but current comments about the city say the Piazza teems with thousands of tourists. After Venice, we crossed into the middle of the country to visit Florence. We saw classical art at the Uffizi Gallery and Michelangelo's famous "David" at another. Florence (*Firenze* in Italian) was also home to many famous sculptures, including the Fountain of Neptune at the Piazza dela Signoria, which included a much greater than life-size naked figure sculpted in great detail that brought some raised eyebrows among the ladies. Our bus then headed for the capital and most historic city of Rome.

    We spent a few days there seeing the sights and traveling in the area. Among the most fascinating were the crumbled but striking ruins of the Roman Colosseum and the classic lines of Vatican City. At the Vatican we visited St. Peter's Basilica and saw the high altar, supposedly built over the tomb of Simon Peter, one of Jesus' apostles. We also wandered through one of Rome's many catacombs and got an up-close look at the Trevi Fountain, full of coins tossed in as depicted in the movie "Three Coins in the Fountain." Another movie that helped make the fountain famous carried the title "Three Coins in the Fountain." Another movie that helped make the fountain famous carried the title "La Dolce Vita." We traveled next to Pisa and climbed the nearly 300 steps (I did, not Alma) in the renowned Leaning Tower. They closed it a few years later for work to stabilize it from leaning further. We drove on around the coast to Monte Carlo in the tiny city-state of Monaco. Our tour group went into the famous casino, but I didn't stay long. I had my camera hung around my neck, and when I got inside, a very serious looking fellow who identified himself as security approached me and said I would have to turn in my camera. For some reason that irked me, and I said I couldn't do that. He promptly grabbed my arm and ushered me out. I've been thrown out of better places. The following morning, our bus headed north through France and finally crossed the channel to England.

We lingered a few days in London where we visited Buckingham Palace, drove around the Houses of Parliament and its iconic clock called Big Ben, and crossed the famous London Tower Bridge. We also viewed the crown jewels at the Tower of London and took a boat ride on the River Thames. Beside the London guides, we had our own source of inside information in Betty McClellan. A native of Edinburgh, Scotland, she had worked in London during World War II, which was where she met Jim, a native Tennessean. While in London, we took a bus tour to the city of Bath, known for its natural hot springs and 18th-century Georgian architecture. We visited a museum built over the original Roman-era Baths, which we saw after descending a stairway. Leaving Bath, we drove to the site of Stonehenge, a prehistoric monument that includes standing stones that form a ring. Archaeologists say work on the stone designs began in 2600 B.C. Some of the stones weighed up to 50 tons and were carried from up to 150 miles away. I don't recall how, but it wasn't easy.

It made quite a spectacle. When we returned to London, we repacked our bags for the flight back to the U.S.

One of my earliest employees at *Nashville Magazine* had a friend who was an ex-FBI agent. We had kept in touch, and it was around this time that he agreed for me to write a book about his life. Jim Scott, or Scotty, had quite a story to tell. I used him as a model for the background of Burke Hill, the main character in my Post Cold War Political Thriller Trilogy. I recorded a long session with Jim about his life in the FBI but lost the tapes in my succession of moves over the last several years. However, the gist of his story appears in Chapter 9 of *Beware the Jabberwock*. According to Jim Scott, he went to Washington just out of high school and got a job working for legendary FBI Director J. Edgar Hoover. He served as sort of a personal delivery boy for Hoover. During this time, the FBI helped him get his college degree in accounting. He then became a special agent. He served in Hoover's "Goon Squad," which carried out black operations of questionable legality, some in foreign countries. One story he told involved a potion dreamed up by the lab guys at Dugway Proving Ground in Utah. He said an agent picked up a sample and was believed to have opened it from curiosity. The agent was found a day or two later wandering around naked and babbling like the village idiot. The Bureau put out word that he'd had a breakdown and resigned. The final chapter in Scott's career devastated him. He said Hoover had obsessed over the FBI's inability to crack the mob. Hoover and Associate Director William Sullivan came up with a plan for Scott to supposedly break with the Bureau and join the underworld. He would keep in contact through Sullivan. He went to Las Vegas and attempted every devious plan he could dream up but didn't manage to get inside the mob. When he came back to Washington after several months, he tried to get in to see Hoover, whom he had always idolized. But the director refused to see him. He had disowned Scott for failing at the assignment. It was quite a tale, and I might have questioned Scott's bona fides, but he gave me copies of correspondence with the FBI where he had requested a copy of his file. A letter from the chief of the Freedom of Information-Privacy Acts Section of the Bureau said they had 500 pages of records but they would not necessarily release all of them. Before we got any further with the project, my former colleague and Scott both moved on. A few years later I heard that he had died.

During this period, I attended the Institute for Organization Management at the University of Delaware sponsored by the U.S. Chamber of Commerce. Our group included organization management professionals from over the eastern U.S. In addition to classes dealing with management, we heard speakers who advised us on matters of personal interest. One talked about investing in rental real estate. After I returned home, I looked into the subject a bit deeper and decided it was time to act. Only a few months from the big six-oh, I had done no investing for the future. The speaker had suggested buying FHA repossessions, which could be had at bargain prices. I bought my first house in July of 1985, a small single family home in the Nashville suburb of Antioch. I paid $45,640 for the foreclosed property. Today a similar foreclosure in the same area is available for about $127,000. I arranged a $60,000 credit line with our house as security in December of 1986 to provide funds for down payments as I moved ahead. Over the next few years I bought a total of thirteen properties, both single family and duplexes. I rented and then sold them over the next several years, but I had a long-term renter in a house in Hendersonville that I kept for about twenty years. The decade continued to move along smoothly, and in 1987 TALU let me take an extra week's vacation for a month-long Far East tour. Alma and I joined our son Mark, an Army Special Forces officer, and his wife I Pun (the I is pronounced as a long "e"), a Korean girl he had married during a previous tour serving just below the Demilitarized Zone with North Korea. He met her on a bus where she used him to practice her English. They were waiting for us at her parents' home in Inchon, South Korea. Alma and I flew commercial to San Francisco, then crossed the bay to Travis Air Force Base. Retired military could fly space available on flights to anywhere for a small fee, $15 back then. It required waiting in the passenger area each time they scheduled a flight, hoping it was headed where you wanted to go. After a couple of days, a bulbous C-5 came in, destination Tokyo. Above its monstrous cargo space rows of seats provided accommodations for a limited number of passengers. Some remained available, and we took off for the Far East. After a stop in Hawaii and overnighting on Guam, we landed at an air base in the Tokyo area. We waited several hours before boarding a C-141 en route to South Korea. There we landed at Suwon, about twenty miles south of Seoul, location of the Eighth Fighter-Interceptor Wing during the Korean War. We arrived late in the afternoon and spent the night at a motel, which was in itself an interesting experience.

    The next morning we took a bus into downtown Seoul where we met Mark at a hotel. We journeyed to Inchon and met I Pun's parents, neither of whom spoke English. Old fashioned Koreans, they wore traditional dress and sat on the floor heated by flues beneath the house called *ondol*. They ate off a small table only a few inches tall. Mark and I Pun had their two boys with them, the youngest just under two. The next day we walked around downtown Seoul and into an area of shops where we bought souvenirs. I found it quite a different experience from my earlier visit in 1952-3. I saw no signs there had ever been a war there. The highlight of our Korea visit took place at a wedding chapel where Mark and I Pun repeated their vows before a Korean minister and a roomful of relatives and friends. I Pun looked radiant in her wedding dress. Mark wore his Army uniform. After the ceremony, some of her girlfriends joined us in a visit to the Inchon waterfront, where MacArthur's troops landed in 1950 behind the invading North Koreans and Chinese in an attempt to cut them off. We walked around the docks and wandered through a ship.

When we caught a flight out of Korea, the two boys stayed behind. We flew to Okinawa, where Mark and I Pun lived close to Mark's Army base. He led an A-Team that had been training Thai Special Forces. We caught a flight at the nearby Kadena Air Base bound for Singapore. The small nation has been developed more, but it appeared a sparkling jewel then as well. We visited Raffles Hotel where a bartender created the Singapore Sling. We also trooped along Orchard Road and its array of shops. We visited a most unusual site called the Tiger Balm Gardens. Developed by two Burmese brothers who moved to Singapore and created Tiger Balm, the theme park featured more than 1000 giant statues and 150 dioramas. They depicted stories of Chinese mythology and folklore including the garish Ten Courts of Hell. It has undergone several transformations and name changes since then but is still known as Tiger Balm Gardens. Its namesake pain reliever is available everywhere, even at Target and Walmart. Our journey encountered a bit of difficulty about the time we were ready to leave Singapore. I Pun lost her passport. Alma and I took a flight out to Thailand, while Mark stayed behind to help get I Pun's situation resolved. They ended up taking a train through Malaysia and up the Thai coast to Bangkok.

Mark knew the sprawling, noisy city of Bangkok well. Our hotel sat out from the center of the city. The morning after Mark and I Pun joined us, he suggested we go for a walk. I don't know if his military background or his high school sport of cross country running set his pace, but I had a problem keeping up. We covered what seemed like a couple of miles in one direction, then made a left turn and strode another mile or two into downtown. Hardly the city of modern roadways and skyscrapers it is today, Bangkok looked more, well, Asian back then. We wandered about some shops, including one with a display of weapons including pistols and knives. We saw buildings with typical Thai architecture, including stepped roofs with curved, spike-like ornaments soaring up from every peak. On the way back we passed the Grand Palace, where kings of Siam had lived for centuries. On another day we took a bus tour of Buddhist temples, including Wat Pho, temple of the Reclining Buddha. The giant Buddha measured 43 meters (141 feet) long, its torso covered in gold leaf. We also got our baptism in the wildness of Bangkok traffic. Besides hordes of cars and trucks, swarms of tuk-tuks joined the mix. To the uninitiated, tuk-tuks are based on a motorcycle, a three-wheeler with a front seat for the driver and a back seat for passengers. We rode them later in our journey. Before leaving Bangkok, we had to take a trip out to Kanchanaburi to see the Bridge on the River Kwai, having seen the movie that came out in 1957. Following a few days in the capital, we boarded a plane for Chiang Mai in mountainous northern Thailand.

After getting situated at Top North Guest House, which featured tiny rooms with plenty of outside exposure, we wandered into town and found a restaurant to eat dinner. By the time we strolled toward the ancient city center, surrounded by a moat, darkness had begun to set in. Mark, quite familiar with the town, led us to the Night Bazaar, where a structure filled with small shops had just begun to come to life with women dressed in typical Thai garb. Don't remember what we bought, but we had an interesting evening. The next day we hailed a *songthaew*, a red pickup truck with benches in the back for passengers. It took us to the base of a mountain peak where we found a steep staircase with 306 steps that would take us to the top, where Wat Phra That Doi Suthep sat. One of northern Thailand's most sacred temples, established in 1383, the monastery could be reached also, fortunately for us, by a funicular lift. However, we did walk down. A terrace at the top featured breadfruit trees, rock gardens, small shrines, and monuments. They included a replica of the white elephant legend says carried a sliver of Buddha's shoulder bone and wandered around the mountain until it died at the spot where they built the temple.

We saw plenty of the huge beasts at an elephant farm not far from Chiang Mai, where they paraded them around. I Pun, always willing to try anything, rode one of the pachyderms. Another day when we went to a nearby village full of craft factories and showrooms, we passed a man riding an elephant along the road. The area had teak wood forests, and we visited a shop where they made teak furniture. You could order a piece and have it shipped to the U.S. We also stopped at a factory where they made gaily-painted paper umbrellas. We bought several and brought them home. When it came time to leave, we boarded a plane for Bangkok, where we changed to Cathay Pacific for the flight to Hong Kong.

Landing at Kai Tak International Airport proved a spectacular experience. The runway stuck out in the water of Kowloon Bay, and some passengers referred to the landing as the "Kai Tak heart attack." I found it rather interesting. We checked into our hotel in the Tsim Sha Tsui section of Kowloon across the bay from Hong Kong island. The next morning we strolled about the stores and hotels in the area. The Star Ferry landing became our next stop. To describe what came next, I'll quote a paragraph from *Beware the Jabberwock*, the first book in my Post Cold War Political Thriller Trilogy.

"They dropped their fares in the turnstile and walked up the ramp to where a green-and-white ferry boat was about ready to board. With one running every few minutes, there was never much of a wait. They found seats on a bench near the front and watched the spectacular skyline approach slowly across the harbor, a panoramic expanse of gleaming high rise office buildings and apartments stacked stair-step up the side of Victoria Peak. The towering Hongkong Bank headquarters, visible a few blocks beyond the Star Ferry terminal, had cost over five billion dollars to build, making it the most expensive office building in the world. Hong Kong was founded on trade, and these were her proud monuments to it."

I used a lot of my Hong Kong experiences in writing that book. Our visit took place only three years before the timeline in the book. China had not yet taken possession of the British colony. It became obvious when we came upon some cops, who were very British bobbies. We spent some time around the area known as Central, then boarded the venerable Peak Tram for its spectacular 1350 meter (4429 feet) journey up the side of Victoria Peak. The tram had been in operation since 1888 and remained one of the most famous sights of Hong Kong. You got a fabulous view of the island from the Peak. We also visited an apartment in one of the towering apartment buildings on the side of the mountain where a friend's daughter lived. She had quite a view from her windows.

Our Far East odyssey ended when we boarded a flight to the Philippines. When we arrived in Manila, we took a bus to Clark Air Force Base (the U.S. pulled out a few years later) forty miles to the northwest. We split up there, with Mark and I Pun heading to Inchon while Alma and I haunted the operations building hoping to find a flight headed for the U.S. After a few days with nothing in sight and my need to get back to work, we took a bus to the Manila airport. We arrived there late, and with no more flights out until morning, they had shut down operations. Clean-up crews busily wiped benches and mopped floors. When they had finished, the lights dimmed and no one remained but us and a few more people awaiting morning flights. Alma and I stayed up for awhile but finally did like the others and stretched out on benches and slept. We awoke in the morning when things began to bustle. I bought tickets to Tokyo with a connecting flight to San Francisco. We finally made it back home in time for the end of my month-long vacation.

Things moved along with no problems for the rest of that year and through the following spring. The TALU Convention brought the usual change of administrations, but this time the outcome proved different. Much like my experience with *Nashville Magazine*, I encountered a superior I couldn't take. I had enjoyed excellent relations with all the TALU presidents up until that time. The new president had an attitude I didn't like and began doing things I couldn't stomach. For one, he told me to fire my administrative assistant, who had been with me since I set up the office. She could be profane at times, but she did a good job. I told him if he wanted her fired, he would have to do it. Which he did. After some mulling around, I decided I'd had enough. The association operated on a July 1 to June 30 year. When he reached the end of his term, I advised the board that I would be leaving at the end of the following June. I don't remember but I think I called it retiring. It would be five months before my 64th birthday. I offered to stay on for another year in an advisory capacity at half salary. The board agreed, and a few months later they gave Alma and me a going away present, a two-week vacation in Hawaii. At the end of November and first of December in 1988, we flew to the 50th state, all expenses paid.

    We split our time between the islands of Kauai, Maui and Hawaii. On Kauai we gaped at Waimea Canyon, called "The Grand Canyon of the Pacific," spectacular waterfalls, and lush landscapes that helped Kauai earn its moniker of the "Garden Isle." We rented a car on each island, and our first trip on Maui took us around the winding road to the summit of the dormant volcano Haleakala, the island's highest peak at 10,023 feet. We experienced an awesome view from that vantage point. On another day we took a tour in a relatively small vehicle along the eastern coastline to the town of Hana, one of Hawaii's last unspoiled frontiers. The road traversed narrow one-lane bridges, hairpin turns and incredible island views. Covering only 52 miles, it included 620 curves and 59 bridges. The historic whaling village of Lahaina provided another striking location, where the

Everything But The Kitchen Sink

channel between Maui and Lanai, the smallest inhabited island, provided the best view of humpback whales. We saw several bobbing in and out of the water. Our final island stop took us to the "Big Island" of Hawaii. We stayed at Hilo and one of our first visits took us to nearby Maunaloa volcano and its Kilauea Caldera, a large crater you could walk into. Steam rose out of spots all around the crater, and we looked into vents where you could see red-hot lava beneath the surface. Kilauea had been erupting since 1983 and still does. Leaving there, we drove down Chain of Craters Road to the point where we had to stop because lava flowing into the ocean had covered the road ahead. Even at a distance from the plume of steam, we could smell the sulfurous odor of the sulfur dioxide gas coming from the lava. We also visited a black sand beach, whose sand glistened like crystals in the sun.

Chapter Eight

MY LAST JOB

FOR ALL PRACTICAL purposes, July 1, 1989 marked my retirement from TALU. During the next twelve months I worked on a few things the woman who replaced me didn't want to do, but I worked at home and only went into the association office occasionally. I had told my TALU friends that I planned to devote my time to writing fiction when I retired. Using what had been the boys' bedroom, I had set up an office after they moved out. Now I lowered my derriere into the office chair and went about writing fiction with a fervor. I created a few characters I liked and proceeded to crank out a novel titled *Beware the Jabberwock*. A blurb I've used put it this way:

As the Cold War sputters to a close and the Soviet Union disintegrates, international telephone intercepts trigger a CIA investigation into the nebulous codeword "Jabberwock." Burke Hill, whose tarnished FBI career ended years earlier after dismissal by a surly J. Edgar Hoover, is recruited to help an old CIA buddy, Cameron Quinn, whose superiors doubt Jabberwock's dangerous potential. When an accident stops Quinn in Hong Kong, the CIA brass warns Hill to drop the investigation. Knowing Quinn's fears about the operation, Hill and Quinn's daughter, Lorelei, continue the chase. Rogue elements on both sides of the old Iron Curtain work to stop them, along with a relentless Federal bureaucracy.

As the clock ticks down on Jabberwork, Burke and Lori realize they alone are the only hope of stopping a plot to assassinate the American and Russian presidents.

I finished the book in early 1990 and began sending out queries to agents. I received several rejections, but in August a request came to see the manuscript. Toward the end of September, I signed a contract with Marlene Connor of the Connor Literary Agency in New York. An associate of hers handled *Jabberwock*, sending the manuscript out to editors. He got rejections but sent me copies of some encouraging letters. An editor at William Morrow commented that "Campbell's scenario was creepily plausible and nicely audacious," but he pointed out a major problem we faced. "Also, given the speed with which global politics are changing these days, I'm reluctant to take on a thriller this topical--for fear that it would already be out of date by the time it sees print." The staffer responsible for the book left at the end of the year, leaving Marlene Conner to handle it. Shortly after that I finished writing the second book in what I now call my Post Cold War Political Thriller Trilogy. Mrs. Conner declined to take it on until she could sell *Jabberwock*, but she said I could submit it to another agent. She continued sending *Jabberwock* out to a few editors with whom she had a good relationship. One from Harper Collins wrote in late 1991: "I simply can't get over the timeliness of this book (I suppose I should say its prescience, given that it was written before the coup), and Mr. Campbell's deep understanding of the American and Soviet systems is impressive." But he added that Harper Collins's fledging thriller line sought books "quite different from the genre as a whole."

After my son Mark returned to the States from Okinawa, he spent some time at Ft. Benning, Georgia,

Chester D. Campbell

where he received a promotion to major. From there the Army sent him to the University of Hawaii to get his master's degree in international studies. He would then be eligible for a post as a military attaché at an embassy. In July of 1991, Alma and I returned to Hawaii to visit Mark, I Pun and the boys at their home in Honolulu. They would have been quite close to the beach except their rental house sat near a deep drainage ditch that separated them from the waterfront. I had been told recently by my doctor that I should walk for thirty minutes every day. I walked back in the direction away from the beach at a healthy pace and covered a good section of the area. We only stayed a week or two but enjoyed our visit. Two things stand out in my mind from the trip. One involved the small, seemingly ubiquitous gecko lizard. We found them on the walls in Mark's house. They could even walk on the ceiling. But the most exciting thing that happened took place on July 11, 1991–a total solar eclipse. Everyone stood out in the street as the sky darkened. We used a magnifying glass to focus an image of the sun on the side of the house and watched as the moon slowly crossed it. It made quite a memorable event. What made it even more memorable, the date happened to be Alma's 65th birthday.

When we returned home, I found my computer waiting. Having previously finished work on *The Poksu Conspiracy*, book two in the series, I prepared to take Marlene Conner's advice and start looking for a new agent. Here's the blurb that gives a capsule of the story:

The Cold War has ended, but a reliable report reveals a plot that could throw the Far East into turmoil. Burke Hill, clandestine director for a Washington PR firm that's a CIA spinoff, is tasked to find the truth about a secret agreement for Israel to help South Korea develop

Everything But The Kitchen Sink

nuclear weapons. The new Seoul government wants all U.S. troops to leave. After a bomb decimates the North Korean leadership in Pyongyang, Hill finds a diligent Seoul Metropolitan Police detective investigating a series of murders he believes are targeted at civilian leaders who favor close cooperation with America. Captain Yun Yu-sop identifies a ruthless Korean assassin who targets anyone who stands in the way, including Burke Hill.

After I sent out a few queries, *Poksu* found a home at the Maximilian Becker agency. Age 88 at the time, he sounded like an old guy when I talked to him (look who's talking). When I got him on the phone, he'd assure me he was working on it. I later learned he had been born in Cairo and had been in the U.S. since 1929. He had co-produced a Broadway play and represented such authors as Ladislas Farago and Georges Simenon, but he didn't do anything for me. After hearing nothing for a few months, I called his office and got the message that he had died. That was the end of 1992, and Marlene Connor had given up on *Jabberwock*. I now had two unpublished manuscripts stacked on the office floor. I had kept writing, of course, and now had a third book ready titled *Overture to Disaster*. Here's the blurb:

Shortly after the Cold War's end, a secretive cabal of international power brokers buys into a dissident communist scheme that, unknown to them, is designed to trigger a horrific act that will paralyze the U.S. It's a thriller right out of today's headlines, though it took place in the early nineties. The theft of Soviet nerve gas weapons and the fate of a Special Operations helicopter mission to Iran set the stage for a thrill ride across continents as international chicanery gone wild seeks to restore dictatorial rule in the former Soviet Union's republics. Can a disgraced Air Force colonel, a Belarus investigator framed for a murder he didn't commit, and a spymaster suddenly left in the cold stop a disaster that will paralyze the nation's capitol?

Starting in early January 1993 I sent out queries for *Overture,* and when one agency replied in mid-March I thought I'd hit the jackpot. Jay Garon-Brooke Associates, the agency that made John Grisham famous, asked to see the manuscript. Garon's letter said I should hear from them in 60-90 days. On October 4 I wrote Garon inquiring about the status of *Overture,* since I had received nothing in writing beyond notice that the manuscript had arrived. I pointed out that I had been calling the agency every two or three weeks over the last couple of months and had been told such things as:

"It has had two excellent readings. An agent is to take it home and read it this weekend. It looks really good for you."..."It will be taken up at an editorial conference next week."..."Mr. Garon was in California last week, but you should hear something shortly."..."Mr. Garon is out of town but it's on his desk. You should hear something in the next ten days."..."Frankly, I don't know what to tell you. It has had two good reads. I'll let them know you inquired about it."

I finally heard in November from a senior staffer that they liked the manuscript but it needed a line edit by a professional editor. I had no idea where to find a professional editor or what a line edit entailed. She also advised that she had two evaluations that contained details of what needed to be changed. I asked her to send me copies and I would revise the book. Despite the problems, the story resonated with the readers. One of them started the evaluation with this paragraph:

"<u>Overture to Disaster</u> is (a) real page turner. The writer weaves together what at first seems disparate strands into an intriguing and eventually exciting drama of espionage and murder. He makes the possibility of a foreign-backed Coup in the nation's capital seem not only plausible but highly possible, and he does so not only with convincing details but with the slow building of drama between the characters. He takes his time, and it's a joy to watch the slow manipulation of events which lead inexorably to the plot to take control of the government."

After reading the evaluations, I realized the major problems involved overwriting and length. I had never heard of overwriting but learned quickly that it involved such things as overly long descriptions. The manuscript ran more than 600 pages. I went to work on it, cutting words, phrases, sentences, paragraphs, and pages. I eliminated some minor characters and worked to make the others more well-rounded. After going through the manuscript at least five times, I managed to shorten it by 110 pages. The exercise tightened the story and picked up the pace. I returned it to Jay Garon-Brooke at the end of January 1994 and received a five-year contract which I signed the first of April. Riding high at that point, I sent them two more novels I had finished. During the months that followed, I struck up a telephone friendship with a young associate at the agency named Kyle. After a long period of hearing nothing about my manuscripts, I asked the young agent about them. He told me the woman who had sent me the contract, an agency vice president, had put them on the shelf and there they sat. This was well into 1995. He said he would say something to Garon about it, but before he could, Garon suffered a sudden death.

I had been active in our church, serving on the Administrative Board and as Church Historian. In the summer of 1995, I heard talk about a celebration of City Road Chapel's 150th anniversary in 1998. I decided to write its history. The project progressed rather slowly as I worked on it along with my fiction. There were a couple of four-drawer files at church with various records from over the years, and I dug through them with notepad at the ready. I spent time at the Madison branch library, looking into the area's history, and searched through the United Methodist Tennessee Conference Archives downtown. I also interviewed several older members of the church on what they remembered from earlier days.

Meanwhile, my wife's health had deteriorated to the point that she fell frequently. I came home from the grocery one day and found her on the floor. I had to stay with her constantly. In October, our church seniors group planned a trip to New Orleans. Alma's sisters decided that I needed a break and came from Knoxville to stay with her while I went on the trip. The group filled a bus and traveled down the Natchez Trace. We stopped at the Tupelo Visitor Center for a short movie on the Trace, then continued toward New Orleans. I used the trip as a model for one the lead character, Bryce Reynolds, took in my last published novel, *Hellbound,* which I wrote originally about a year later. During the venture, I chanced to spend time on a few occasions with one of my Sunday School class members, Sarah Blankenship, and her friend, June Burgess. We shared a muffuletta at a restaurant and also a French Quarter tour in one of New Orleans' famous mule-driven carriages. More of her later. I described the French Quarter tour in detail in Chapter 25 of *Hellbound*. I had brought a small recorder on the trip and recorded the carriage driver's spiel. I quoted liberally from it in the Novel.

I had made other trips with the church group, including one to St. Simons Island off the coast just east of Brunswick, Georgia. We Methodists had a special link to the island, as it served as a sometimes home in the 1730s for John Wesley, the young Anglican missionary who went back to England and founded the Methodist Church. On a later tour I joined two Sunday School class members, Betty McClellan, our Scottish friend, and Sarah Blankenship, in enjoying visits to New York City, Jamestown, Virginia, and the Greenbrier Hotel at White Sulphur Springs, West Virginia. Besides the iconic luxury resort, we were fascinated by a tour of the Emergency Relocation Center, a bunker or bomb shelter, built by the U. S. government in the 1950's to be occupied by the U.S. Congress in case of war. They constructed the secret underground facility in conjunction with an above ground addition to the hotel, the West Virginia Wing. For thirty years the facility codenamed Project Greek Island remained at a constant state of operational readiness. The end of the Cold War brought a decommissioning of the bunker. We walked through the tunnel that connected the once-secret project to an unobtrusive entrance to the hotel.

Robert Thixton bought the literary agency after Jay Garon's death. and my young contact, Kyle, told him about my manuscripts. Thixton wanted a new title for *Overture to Disaster*. I mentioned it had originally been titled *Red Ruse*, and he suggested *The Deadly Ruse*. In a letter dated October 17, Thixton wrote he had sent it to Forge/TOR books. It brought the usual rejection, we like it, but...I now had another book for submission, *The Cambridge Document*. I sometimes paused but never stopped writing.

In the spring of 1996 I had bigger problems to deal with. They diagnosed my wife with Parkinson's disease. The neurologist who treated her told us of an operation that could neutralize some of the effects of the disease that plagued Alma, such as a tendency to fall, shaky hands, and difficulty eating. It involved inserting two probes through the top of her head and cauterizing spots in her brain. When we talked to the surgeon, he told us there was only a five percent chance of anything going wrong. We discussed the situation and agreed that she should go ahead with the surgery. Her symptoms had been steadily worsening, and the ninety-five percent odds of success tipped the balance. We lived in the Madison suburb, and he performed the surgery at Madison's Nashville Memorial Hospital (now an office rental facility). Some of our kids were with me as we waited for the doctor to come out. When he finally did, he explained that he had stopped the surgery after doing one side as she was showing signs of fatigue and the operation required her to remain conscious and alert, able to reply to questions. He put her in the ICU, and when we got to see her, she seemed groggy and mostly uncommunicative. During the evening she appeared no better. We expressed our concern, but they told us not to worry. The next morning she showed no change, and when the doctor arrived he did a brain scan and said it showed a massive hematoma, a blood clot on one side of her head, putting pressure on the brain. It had left her totally paralyzed, with no ability to speak.

 I transferred her to a rehabilitation hospital near our home. After a couple of weeks, the doctor there said he could do no more for her. She needed to be in a nursing home. I checked her into Imperial Gardens in Madison. I felt both the neurologist and the hospital had been negligent in their care of her. I thought about how some people might sue them both, but what good would it do? Insurance paid all of Alma's medical bills. If I got anything, it would be for some legalese like pain and suffering, and no amount of money could cure that. Anything I received for Alma would do her no good, and I couldn't accept payment for letting her get into this condition. I spent time with her every day in the nursing home. I bought her a TV to watch, and I worked with her in an attempt to get some movement or reaction. She watched the TV and said a word or two on occasion. But after a few months she had a problem that caused them to send her back to the hospital. Anne came home to help. When the hospital released her, I put Alma in her wheelchair and rolled her out to the car. Up to that point she had not said a complete sentence, but this time her words were clear: "I want to go home." I took her back to the nursing home with a heavy heart.

By January 1997 I had completed work on the story I developed from that church trip to New Orleans a little more than a year before. I titled it *Hell Bound*, bundled it up, and sent it off to the agent.

Alma had been in the nursing home for more than a year when I decided the time had come to take her home. I bought a hospital bed and fixed up what had been the girls' bedroom. A few weeks before Christmas in 1997, I brought her back to the house we had lived in the past 32 years. I arranged for a home nursing service to look after her during the day, changing her bed and checking her feeding tube. We moved her to a chair in the living room occasionally. We had a full house for Christmas, including Steve, his wife Gayle, and their two boys; Mark, I Pun, and their two boys; Betsy, her husband Jim, and their daughter and son (they had two more kids later); and Anne. We had our annual get-together with brother Jim's family at our place. Alma sat and watched everything but showed no emotion. Shortly after Christmas, when we were alone again, she began breathing rapidly. I asked the home health nurse about it, and she decided we should transfer Alma to the hospital. The doctor diagnosed her with pneumonia. After a few weeks they pronounced her cured. She had been breathing with a respirator, and they sent her to a rehab hospital across town to wean her off of it. I visited with her daily, and she appeared to be doing well. They took her off the respirator, and when I arrived on Friday morning, they said I could take her home that weekend. While I was preparing supper that evening, I had a call from the rehab hospital. Alma had stopped breathing. They asked if they should attempt to resuscitate her. I said of course. I still couldn't accept that she wouldn't get any better.

When I made it to the hospital, the nurse met me and said, "I'm sorry, we couldn't do anything for her."

I found her lying in her bed as if she were asleep. I kissed her goodbye and held her hand. I sat there for awhile, don't remember how long, just feeling numb. Then I called Anne and asked her to call her sister and brothers.

It was a cold February day, Friday the 13th, 1998.

That same month, with the sesquicentennial celebration just ahead, I finished work on the church history I had started back in 1995 and sent it to the printer. In the end I had a 288-page book that was titled *The Best Is Yet To Be*, which was a favorite saying of our then pastor, Dr. Lynn Hill.

Back in New York, things had gone no better for my manuscripts. The young agent, Kyle, decided to leave Jay Garon-Brooke and form his own agency. He asked if he could represent me. I agreed and pulled my manuscripts from the large agency. On my recommendation, a colleague of mine, Beth Terrell-Hicks, sent her manuscript to my new agent. We talked to him a couple of times, the last time in December of 1998, then nothing. He simply disappeared. We finally heard from another source that he had died. I began to feel like I had been jinxed. My agents were falling like flies. Beth and I had been members of a rather loosely organized critique group for a few years, and she had offered valuable insights regarding my early manuscripts. We have continued to be close colleagues ever since.

In the fall of 1998, my brother asked me to join him on a trip his Sunday School Class from Brentwood United Methodist Church planned for a visit to the Holy Land. We left the first week of November on a nearly two-week journey that took us the length and breadth of the small nation of Israel. Our flight on Royal Jordanian Airlines landed in Amman, Jordan, where we spent the first night. The next morning we boarded a bus for a visit to the ancient city of Petra, where we marveled at the famous facade called The Treasury, carved into the rock face of a cliff in 312 B.C. It was featured in the movie *Indiana Jones and the Last Crusade*. The next morning we toured Mount Nebo, the biblical location from which God allowed Moses to view the Promised Land. Nearby we toured the Greek Orthodox church at Madaba, famous for its mosaics. Then we bid Jordan farewell and headed for the King Hussein (Allenby on the Israeli side) Bridge across the Jordan River.

I never saw a bridge take so long to cross. We sat on the bus while the Jordanian border guards checked us out. Finally we crossed over to the Israeli side where they scrutinized our passports and asked questions. When we finally got underway again, we traveled a short distance into Jericho, one of the oldest cities in the world. We saw where archeologists uncovered twenty successive settlements, the oldest dating back 11,000 years.

Afterward we headed for the Holy City, Jerusalem. That's where we remained for several days, seeing sites in the city and making day trips to nearby areas. Masada proved one of the most spectacular. The flat-topped rock formation rose 1300 feet above the Dead Sea. It had a triple-terrace palace carved out of the rock by Herod the Great around 37 B.C. But it is best known as the site where 960 members of an offshoot of the Jewish Zealots committed suicide in 73 A.D. They chose that outcome rather than capture by Roman soldiers climbing the west wall to attack. We took a cable car to the top, visited the ruins, and marveled at the view of the Dead Sea. We also visited Bethlehem, only a few miles south of Jerusalem, where the magnificent Church of the Nativity contained a grotto marked as the traditional place of Jesus birth. Empress Helena, mother of Constantine the Great, around 327 A.D. identified many other sites in Israel called "traditional" locations of holy places.

We must have visited a dozen churches around Jerusalem marking various spots associated with Jesus' life and ministry. It started as we walked down from the Mount of Olives toward the old walled city. We passed two on the way and another at the bottom of the hill beside the Garden of Gethsemane, where Jesus prayed and his disciples slept the night before his crucifixion. It bore the name Church of All Nations. One of the most interesting tours in the Old City took us to the Wailing Wall, where Orthodox Jews with beards and high hats bowed and prayed. Afterward, we climbed the stairs to the Temple Mount, one of the holiest places of three religions: Christians, Jews, and Muslims. We visited two of the Muslims' most revered sites, the al-Aksa Mosque and the Dome of the Rock. We spent a good while roaming through the Church of the Holy Sepulchre, the

Everything But The Kitchen Sink

largest church we saw in Jerusalem. Portions of it are held by six denominations. We entered on the top level and worked our way down to the main floor where elaborate structures mark what are considered by the six denominations to be locations of both the crucifixion and Jesus' tomb. On another tour, I found the Shrine of the Book a quite interesting site. With a roof like a jar cover, it held the Dead Sea Scrolls. Glass cases contained samples of various documents.

Since Palestinian brothers owned the bus line we used, we had been booked into the Ambassador Hotel in the Arab sector of East Jerusalem. Departing the city, we moved through a check point that marked a change from Israeli control to Palestinian control. Heading north, we stopped at Jacob's well, where Jesus spoke to the Samaritan woman at the well. As usual a church had been built over the well. And like so many others it has had a violent history due to conflicts between Christians, Jews, and Muslims. Built in the fourth century, it was destroyed in the seventh, rebuilt by Crusaders in the eleventh, destroyed again in the twelfth, and underwent various attempts at reconstruction in 1860 and 1914 and finally completed in 2007. We passed Meggido, the site of countless battles over the centuries, on the southern edge of the Jezreel Valley, which separates Samaria from the Galilee. The English corruption of Har Meggido, or Meggido Hill, gave us the word Armageddon. We visited countless churches around the Sea of Galilee, which is actually a large lake. We took a ride on a "Jesus Boat," which was supposed to be similar to one he would have sailed aboard. On the northeastern shore we visited a kibbutzim, a tightly communal village with common ownership. Then we traveled up onto the Golan Heights, which was Syrian prior to the Six-Day War in 1967. We saw an old Syrian gun emplacement aimed at the kibbutzim below, left to show the threat that once existed. The Golan is a major agricultural area, though it was never developed by the Syrians.

Leaving the Galilee, we drove toward Haifa, Israel's third largest city. We rode across the Carmel range and saw more trees than I encountered anywhere else in Israel. We saw an Israeli Air Force base down below and beyond that the peak of Mount Hermon, the highest point in the country. We also saw two Druze villages. The Druze are a breakaway sect of Islam who like the Israelis because they are given freedom to worship as they wish. Many of them fought with the Israelis against the Arab invaders. Probably the most striking sight in Haifa was the Bahai Shrine and Gardens, which featured nineteen terraces stretching from the base of Mount Carmel to its summit. Before going down into the main part of the city, we got a great view of the Mediterranean and Haifa's port facilities.

We took the coastal road south and made our first stop at the ancient Roman port of Caesarea, which had been destroyed and rebuilt several times. We wandered around the port area and the town that included an outdoor Roman theatre. Our guide pointed out its superior acoustics by standing on the stage and speaking in a normal voice, which to us on the ground below sounded as if amplified. After overnighting at Netanya in a hotel that faced the sea, we motored into Tel Aviv, Israel's second largest city. We toured the downtown area, then our bus parked near St. Peter's Church within walking distance of the old port of Jaffa. We tramped around a warren of stone walkways leading to artists' studios and small shops built on several levels above the seashore. One place was identified as the location where

Saint Peter stayed while in Jaffa. When we headed back to our bus, we had to negotiate a line of cars and vans displaying olive wood figures and other trinkets. I used this in a key scene in *Secret of the Scroll,* my first Greg McKenzie mystery. We left Jaffa for the drive to Jerusalem, then headed on to Amman, Jordan for our return to the U.S. During the flight home, I read an article in the Royal Jordanian Airlines magazine about an archeological dig in the ancient settlement of Bethany in Jordan, where they found evidence of Christian monks living in caves during the first few centuries.

Back home I sat in my office and began digesting all the information I had brought with me. As I reviewed the article in the airline magazine, a plot began to take shape in the way they always do. What if someone found an ancient scroll in one of those caves around Bethany? And what would be in the scroll that could cause considerable upheaval? All those what if questions sent me digging further. And before long, I had the outline of a story and some characters that wound up on the page as *Secret of the Scroll*, a thriller that took place about half in Nashville and half in the Holy Land. It involved a mountain of research, including reading half a dozen library books on subjects such as the Bible Codes, a number of interviews both by phone and in person, and travel to several locations. Greg McKenzie, my main character, had retired as an Air Force Office of Special Investigations major. When I finished the manuscript in June of 1999, I mailed a copy to the former agent in charge of the OSI at Arnold Air Force Base south of Nashville, who I had interviewed earlier. He sent back some useful suggestions. I started sending out queries to agents in August, and after about thirty rejections, some of which commented that I had a great idea but "it doesn't suit our needs," I received one from an agent in Dallas who subsequently read the manuscript and suggested I send it to a professional editor. I complied and made a major overhaul on the book. I sent it back to the agent in mid-2000. After several months, I received a letter from the agent saying she no longer handled fiction but had given the manuscript to her husband, John Lewis, who ran Durban House, a small publisher in Dallas. By early 2001 I had a contract calling for publication of three books. It had an unusual feature that I was not familiar with but accepted. Rather than paying me anything up front, Durban House charged me a fee the contract said covered things like promotion and marketing, not publishing. They did some promotion and marketing but nothing like what I paid for. After the long process of typesetting, revisions, page proofs, corrections, and design, I finally became a published author with book in hand in October of 2002. Here's the blurb:

Deadly groups of Palestinians and Israelis struggle to gain possession of an ancient parchment scroll that was unknowingly brought back to the States from the Holy Land by retired Air Force investigator Greg McKenzie. When his wife is taken hostage, he finds himself mired in the duplicitous world of Middle East politics and religion. He is forced to mount his own black operation inside Israel in the search for his wife.

Meanwhile, back in Madison other things had been going on. In May of 1999, after mulling things over between bouts at the computer with the nearly-finished *Secret of the Scroll*, I invited Sarah Blankenship out to dinner. You may remember her as my Sunday School classmate from the church tours back in the earlier nineties. We also took in a movie one evening and went on other dates. Seven years younger than me, she had reached her mid-sixties. We enjoyed each other's company and got along well. She had lost two husbands and knew what I had gone through with Alma. At my age I saw no reason to piddle around. In late June I invited her to my house for dinner, which I prepared. Afterward, we sat on the living room sofa, and I asked her to marry me. She seemed shocked at first, but then accepted the engagement ring I proffered. I had planned a get-together with my kids and wives and husbands in Gatlinburg for early July, and I broke the news of my impending marriage there. They all seemed happy with the idea. And on September 4, 1999, Sarah and I took our vows at City Road Chapel United Methodist Church in Madison with only our close family members present. We headed east on our honeymoon, spending the first night in Gatlinburg. From there we drove to Maggie Valley on the North Carolina side of the Smokies, where we spent a night or two. We wound up in the backwoods outside Asheville at a place called Mountain Springs Cabins and Chalets. We stayed there for nearly a week and enjoyed the outdoors and the fresh air.

We were home only a short time when another trip came up. This one lasted only about a week and involved the same travel agent who had booked tours like the one I had taken to Europe with the McClellans. She promoted it as a Tulip Festival tour, but when we got to Holland, Michigan, a storm had just decimated the tulip crop. We saw a few blooms around, but most fields appeared virtually bare. The bus took us to Upper Michigan, where we boarded a boat for Mackinac Island near the Mackinac Straits which separate Lake Huron from Lake Michigan. We stayed at the magnificent Grand Hotel that sat on a hill with a marvelous view. While there a couple of days, we strolled about the row of shops down at the lakeside.

Sarah found the candy store particularly enticing. After leaving the island, our bus took us back to Tennessee.

As soon as I finished with *Secret of the Scroll*, I started work on another novel. I had lived with Greg and Jill McKenzie for over a year and had become quite fond of them. I decided to turn their lives into a series. I began the way I normally do, with an idea for a beginning and a vague idea of how it would end. I started the story in Nashville but chose the Pensacola, Florida area for the major action. After Sarah and I married, we began spending a couple of weeks each spring and fall at brother Jim's condo on the Gulf beach at Perdido Key, just west of Pensacola. I did a lot of writing while there. In this case, I did most of the research for *Designed to Kill*, the first Greg McKenzie whodunit, while there. I did interviews with a National Parks ranger, a medical examiner, a forensics investigator, a building inspector, a sheriff's department investigator, and, after getting back home, a civil engineer friend, plus my trusted engineering consultant, brother Jim.

In August of 2000, not long after I sent the revised *Secret of the Scroll* back to the agent, Sarah and I left on another journey called Grand European Odyssey, this one promoted by our pastor. Betty McClellan also joined us. Dr. Hill led our section of the trek booked by Educational Opportunities Tours. We flew from Nashville to Washington Dulles on August 29 and landed in Paris the following morning. Staying there for three days, we visited such sights as the Arc de Triomphe, the Eiffel Tower (great view of Paris), the Louvre, and Notre Dame Cathedral. We also took a nighttime boat ride on the Seine and visited the ornate Palace of Versailles just southwest of Paris. The incident Sarah remembers best was the pastor holding open the door to a unisex restroom with a big grin. "Come on in, ladies," he said. We traveled next to Luxembourg, where we visited the American military cemetery. Wandering around the graves, we found the burial place of Gen. George S. Patton, Jr., who led the 3rd Army and was instrumental in the liberation of Germany in World War II. His name also appears on a street in the subdivision where we now live. We motored on to Frankfurt, Germany, and strolled around the downtown area, where we bought a few souvenirs.

We headed next to Heidelberg, where we visited the ruins of Heidelberg Castle, one of Europe's oldest, started early in the 14th century. Damaged by lightning and a succession of wars, the castle underwent rebuilding projects several times but remains mostly ruin. Despite this, it stands spectacularly on a hillside above the Old Town and attracts thousands of visitors. We also toured the baroque Old Town with its stone bridge over the Neckar River. Leaving Heidelberg, we traveled down the Romantic Road through towns like Nordlingen and Dinkelsbuhl to our evening's destination of Oberammergau. A picturesque town in the Bavarian Alps, it featured shops and hotels with decorated windows and gaily painted art. But the town's claim to fame came the following day when we attended its once-a-decade production of the Passion Play. Betty and I had seen it earlier on my first trip to Europe.

Our Grand Odyssey continued the next day when we crossed the Alps to Innsbruck, Austria. In the city's Old Town we saw the famous Golden Roof, a five-story building with the roof of an alcove balcony covered with more than 6,500 fire-gilded copper tiles put there by Emperor Maximilian I around 1500. We gazed at the 28 life-size bronze statues in Hofkirche, or Court Church, who guarded Maximilian's tomb, although old Max had been moved to another site. Other sights we viewed included Maria Theresa's Palace and the Triumphal Arch. We traveled next to Bern, the Swiss capital, which was built on a peninsula surrounded by the Aare River. It had spilled over to the other side of the river, but we visited the old part where the government was located. In the afternoon our bus took us south to the mountainside village of Leysin, where we would make our evening home for the next five nights.

Morning brought us to Geneva and tours of the U.N. Palace and St. Pierre's Cathedral. We took a boat ride on Lake Geneva, the largest lake in Western Europe. The following day found us journeying through the Rhone River Valley to Tasch, where we boarded a train to Zermatt, the mile-high mountain resort with a view of the pyramid-shaped colossus called the Matterhorn. In Zermatt we changed to a rack railway that took us to the summit of the Gornergrat at 10,135 feet. There we had a great view of the snow-covered Matterhorn, which rises to 14,692 feet. Our viewing area did not cover much ground, and Sarah, who has a problem with heights, wouldn't venture anywhere close to the edge.

The next two days were a bit better as we stuck to places we could travel strictly by bus. At Gruyeres we toured the Gruyeres Castle, one of the oldest and most popular in Switzerland, and we sampled Gruyere cheese where it was made. From there we visited Chateau de Chillon, or Chillon Castle, built on a rocky islet beside the shore of Lake Geneva. Considered by some the prettiest castle in Switzerland and one of the most visited in Europe, Chillon owes its fame largely to Lord Byron and his poem "The Prisoner of Chillon," which appeared in 1816. Chillon got its start as a Roman outpost, and the earliest record appeared in 1005. We roamed about the castle and down to its dungeon, where we saw signs made by its most famous prisoner dragging his chain. We visited nearby Lausanne and Montreux, where we spent the night. The next day our bus took us on to Interlaken, where we stopped briefly in the town built between two lakes (hence the name Interlaken), Brienz, then Lucerne. We found Lucerne most interesting. Our hotel resided in the Old Town with its medieval architecture. We strolled a nearby covered bridge, built in 1333, across the Reuss River to the modern side. The city fronted on Lake Lucerne, with views of mountains in the distance. Of course, mountains loomed everywhere in Switzerland.

In the morning, we boarded the bus on the first leg of our journey home. We returned to Heidelberg, then continued to Frankfurt. When we got to the airport the next day, I saw across the field a U.S. Air Force air transport unit, the same type of organization I had worked with in the Air National Guard. On the afternoon of September 13, we boarded a United flight to Chicago O'Hare. It had been an eventful two weeks, but it was time to get back to the book business.

When I received *Secret of the Scroll* in October 2002, I realized the work had just begun. If I intended to make any money and become known, I would have to promote the book and sell it. I ordered books from the publisher and began setting up signings. I arranged one of the first for Books-a-Million (BAM) not far from our home in Madison. Sarah joined me at the signing table at the front of the store. Some of our church members bought books, but most of the buyers had never heard of me and were surprised to find a local author. I sold thirty or so books and was elated. I began to branch out, doing signings at BAM stores across the state in Murfreesboro, Jackson, Memphis, Oak Ridge, Knoxville, and Johnson City. I designed a small leaflet promoting the book, and Sarah passed them out at the front of the stores. When I mentioned what we were doing on an Internet writers' list, some of them had never heard of this tactic and decided it was a great idea to emulate.

By early 2002, I had sent the completed manuscript of *Designed to Kill* to Durban House. I began working on edits in the middle of 2002 with Bob Middlemiss, an excellent editor who provided significant help,. The mills of publishing grind exceedingly slow, and they did not get around to asking my help with the book cover until the following spring. Meanwhile, I had been attending writers' conferences including Sleuthfest, the premier offering of the Florida Chapter of Mystery Writers of America. Phillip Margolin, a *New York Times* bestseller, spoke at one of the sessions. At one point he said don't be afraid to approach other authors for cover blurbs. I took his advice and contacted him about writing one for *Designed to Kill*. He agreed. I dummied up an ARC (Advance Review Copy) using my laser printer and sent it to him. Durban House wound up using his comment in a circular, seal-like piece of art on the front cover. I kept doing book signings around Tennessee later in 2003, branching out into Kentucky and Alabama. We visited my son Steve in Pennsylvania, and I did signings at a Barnes & Noble in Camp Hill and at the Mechanicsburg Mystery Book Store. In October we attended Bouchercon, one of the largest mystery conferences, in Las Vegas. On the way we did signings in Hattiesburg and Pass Christian, Mississippi. On the way back we signed at San Antonio and Plano, Texas. In between all this I had finished work on the third book in the Greg McKenzie series and sent the manuscript to Durban House's editor on April 28. But I needed to concentrate my efforts at the moment on getting everything ready for the launching of *Designed to Kill*.

With the prospect of having two books on the market, I looked around for a way to smooth the path. In December I signed up with Patti Nunn of Breakthrough Promotions to help with promotion and marketing. I finally received copies of the new book in March of 2004, with its official release on April 1. Here's the blurb:

It's no vacation that brings Greg McKenzie and his wife, Jill, to the glistening white sand beaches at Perdido Key, Florida. Architect Tim Gannon, son of the McKenzies' closest friends, is found dead of a gunshot wound. Self-inflicted, says the deputy who investigated, a clear case of remorse over a design flaw in a beachfront condo that caused a balcony collapse, killing two people. It looks otherwise to Greg and Jill, who find plans missing, an obstinate contractor, a too-slick developer, and an inspector angry over a disrupted love affair. After two hoods work him over, Greg realizes Jill is in danger, too, and if this is a murder case, he had better solve it without delay.

In May, with a new book to sell, we returned to the two Pennsylvania bookstores and also scheduled two signings around our twice-a-year digs on Perdido Key. The mail brought an invitation to submit my information to appear in *Who's Who in America*. After that my bios continued to appear for years in either *Who's Who in America* or *Who's Who in The World*. During that summer we kept up our signing routine, including two in Clarksville, two in the Chattanooga area, and our fourth time at the Madison BAM. Whenever I landed at home long enough to accomplish anything, I worked back and forth with Durban House Editor Bob Middlemiss on edits of *Deadly Illusions*. It finally went to the typesetter on

Chester D. Campbell

August 19. September found us in Atlanta for the Southeast Booksellers Association, with bookstore owners to meet and books to give them. Sort of like priming the pump. We headed west again after that, driving I-40 all the way from Nashville to where it ended at Barstow, California. With the help of a friend in Orange County, I had set up several signings at bookstores just below Los Angeles. We hit a Borders in Rancho Santa Margarita, Barnes & Noble in Aliso Viejo, Borders in Orange, and another Borders at Costa Mesa. Between the signings we attended the annual Men of Mystery event in Irvine, where the writers were split up and seated at tables with readers.

Shortly after we returned from California, we hit the road again and drove I-40 to it's eastern end near Cape Fear, North Carolina, where we took in the Cape Fear Crime Festival. During the rest of October and November, we did two more events, including the Kentucky Book Fair, where we sold stacks of books. We closed out 2004 with signings each Saturday leading up to Christmas while touting books as gifts. I was told most authors avoided this period *because* of Christmas. Summing up my efforts, I did 23 radio interviews in 2004. Since starting with *Secret of the Scroll* and adding *Designed to Kill*, I had done 68 book signings through 2004.

In the early part of 2005, I cut down on bookstore signings and spent more time on special events and writers' conferences. I continued doing interviews set up by Patti Nunn. In January I spoke to the Downtown Nashville Lions Club and later did events like a senior center flea market and a scheduled signing at the Madison Station Senior Center. Copies of the paperback version of *Deadly Illusions* finally appeared at my doorstep on April 26. Here's the book blurb:

Everything But The Kitchen Sink

A young woman named Molly Saint hires Greg and Jill McKenzie to check her husband's background, then disappears. It starts them on a tangled trail of deceit, with Jill soon turning up a close family connection. Complicating matters further, Greg gets drawn into a troubling police investigation stemming from the assassination of the Federal Reserve Board chairman at a Nashville hotel. The deeper the McKenzies dig, the more illusions they face. Nothing appears to be what it seemed at first, and after arson, break-ins and threats, they face a deadly confrontation.

I now had three books to sell at signings. I took time out from the murder and mayhem business in mid-June to serve as a delegate from City Road Chapel to the Annual Conference of the United Methodist Church's Tennessee Conference. Then it was back to the mystery pursuit. I stepped up my activity in July, setting up a string of appearances starting in south Alabama and heading down to Perdido Key. They began with a store in Thomasville, Alabama on July 7. The following afternoon we had a signing in Mobile from two to four. Unfortunately, our timing turned out to be terrible. We arrived at the store a little early and set up our table with plenty of books. We made a few sales although we didn't see many customers in the store. After awhile, the manager came over with a worried look.

"They report Hurricane Dennis has hit Cuba with winds of 135 to 145 miles per hour and is headed this way," she said. "They're starting to evacuate people along the coast."

This was on Friday. We were scheduled to be in Bay St. Louis, Mississippi the next day, and I figured that was out. We decided to hit nearby I-65 and head toward home. Since my watch showed nearly 3:30 p.m., I called ahead and made a reservation at a motel in Birmingham. When we got to the interstate, we wedged our way into a solid stream of traffic headed north. Instead of the usual 70 mph (or more) speed, we alternated between creeping along and moving in spurts of 50 to 60 mph. We reached our motel in Birmingham at nine o'clock– a distance of 258 miles at an average speed of about 47 mph. When we checked in at the motel, it became obvious that I had done the right thing in making a reservation. Other people flocked in only to be told no rooms were available.

Early in August we did a three-day tour in Upper East Tennessee and just across the border in Virginia. The following week we headed back to Pennsylvania to combine four days of signings with grandson Dan Campbell's wedding. The week after that, we did another event at the Nashville Public Library's Main Branch, then headed to Knoxville for a signing and a Skill Build I had arranged for members of the Southeast Chapter of Mystery Writers of America (SEMWA) in the area. I had been elected West District Representative for the states of Tennessee, Alabama, and Mississippi, a post I held for three years.

October brought a short stay at our Perdido Key hideaway, from which we did a few signings to replace those cancelled by Hurricane Dennis. We took in another writers' conference at the end of the month, one we attended on several occasions in Muncie, Indiana called Magna cum Murder. In November we returned to the Kentucky Book Fair, which always provided an opportunity to sell lots of books. We did our lead up to Christmas on two Saturdays, first at BAM in Murfreesboro, then the Clarksville BAM. I had been working on a new book that would be the fourth in the Greg McKenzie series, and with the dawning of 2006 I stepped up my efforts to finish it. Spending more time on church work and school activities with Sarah's third grade grandson, Justin Jones, who now lived with us, I curtailed my book signing activities. I also realized I had not been getting anything from my signing efforts for quite awhile. My last royalty check from Durban House had been received in December 2004, which meant I had been paid little for *Designed to Kill* and nothing for *Deadly Illusions*. When I put my pencil to it, I found I had received payment for a little under 2000 books. But Durban House had print runs of that much on each of the three books. At the Men of Mystery event in California I had met two other Durban House authors who were not happy with the way they had been treated. I contacted Ben Small and Chris Holmes by phone, and we decided to set up a session with John Lewis. I flew to Dallas on March 11, where we confronted John and his wife, who admitted there had been problems and made all kinds of promises regarding how they would do better. Ben, Chris and I had dinner afterward and agreed we had little faith in the promises. We decided to keep in touch.

I finished the first draft of book four, titled *The Marathon Murders*, in April. That month also ended my real estate career when I closed on the last house in Hendersonville. I did an occasional signing along the way with books I had left. In June I began to send out queries for *The Marathon Murders*. I sent most of them to a long list of agents and others to small presses. Sarah and I attended the ConMisterio conference in Austin, Texas in July, and we did two events in September, the Midwest MysteryFest in St. Charles, Missouri and Bouchercon in Madison, Wisconsin. As usual, when I finished writing one book, I started on another. As I mentioned in a *Crimespree Magazine* article, sometimes you feel like doing something different. After four books involving Greg and Jill McKenzie, I had a hankering to do something more hard-boiled. I created a PI named Sid Chance with a checkered background. He operated out of Madison, where Sarah and I lived. I returned to my desk and began writing again. Early October found me on my back in the hospital for nearly a week, thanks to pancreatitis. We hit the road a couple of weeks later for a return to Magna cum Murder in Muncie, Indiana. That completed our travels for the year.

Finding no changes in my relationship with Durban House (such as books not getting shipped for signings), I wrote in January 2007 requesting that my rights be returned for all of my books. In return I agreed to release DH from all claims for royalties unpaid. I finally received a Settlement and Release in September. I sent it to Ben Small (both he and his wife were lawyers) and Rebecca returned it with a few suggested changes to level the playing field. I signed the document and forwarded it to DH in early October. This was also the time that I sent Durban House a check for $1750 to cover 400 copies of *Deadly Illusions* and 100 of *Secret of the Scroll*, which would be shipped from the distributor in the middle of November. Also during this period Ben and I put together an independent mystery publisher we named Night Shadows Press. We planned it to take care of orphaned authors like us. Its first book would be *The Marathon Murders*. Our next problem was to find a small press that could handle printing and distribution. Somebody suggested Wingspan Press, and I contacted them in December, setting up an account and arrangements for our first book.

Meanwhile, on a personal level, Sarah's granddaughter, Brandy Metcalf, planned a beach

Everything But The Kitchen Sink

wedding at Destin, Florida in May, and we stopped at nearby Niceville for a signing. We did something different in July, taking a short vacation in the Great Smoky Mountains with no connection to books. In August we attended the inaugural session of Killer Nashville, a writers' conference that has grown into one of the major mystery events in the U.S. We did Magna cum Murder again in October, as well as a signing at the VFW Octoberfest in Nashville neighbor Hendersonville. We also took another strictly personal trip, a six-day cruise out of Mobile to Cancun, Mexico.

In February of 2008 I held a launch party for *The Marathon Murders* at, where else, the old Marathon Motor Works just beyond downtown Nashville. We served punch and such for invited guests in the showroom complete with a shiny 1912 Marathon touring car.

Barry Walker, a dynamic entrepreneur, bought the old Marathon buildings in a blighted area off Charlotte Avenue back in the 1980's. He learned that the three-story office building on one side of the street had been the headquarters of Marathon Motor Works in the early part of the twentieth century. The factory building stood across the street. The Marathon became a highly popular car, and the newspapers predicted it would make Nashville a center of the automotive industry. But mistakes by key executives quickly doomed the company. Walker had unearthed a lot of the history when refurbishing the office building. He called his restoration Marathon Village. When I read about it at the library, a plot took shape. Walker gave me the run of the place while I wrote the book, and he told his story to those attending the book launch party. Of course, I threw in a few murders to liven up the pages. Here's the book blurb:

Senior P.I.'s Greg and Jill McKenzie take on a 90-

year-old murder case, dragging them into a present day conspiracy. Three new murders appear aimed at suppressing the secret behind 1914 records of Nashville's defunct Marathon Motor Works. Their clients, Col. Warren Jarvis and his girlfriend, Kelli Kane, think her great-great-grandfather, a Marathon officer charged with embezzlement, was framed and murdered. A Tennessee Bureau of Investigation agent doubts the new crimes involve their case. Then Kelli disappears. A rich socialite distracts Greg, but everything pales at the dire straits he finds himself in when he comes face-to-face with the murderer.

With another book in my sales inventory, and a backlist supply from Durban House's distributor, I began setting up signings again. At the end of February and first of March I did signings in Florida in connection with attending SleuthFest. Night Shadows Press published Ben Small's second mystery, *The Olive Horseshoe*, in May. That month also took us back to Pennsylvania for grandson Andrew's wedding and a couple of return signings. We made another visit to one of our favorite areas in June, signing at a Montgomery, Alabama Barnes & Noble on our way to three signings in Pensacola. We included what had become our favorite library, the Southwest Branch just north of Perdido Key in Pensacola. October brought the first event in what became a steady stream of joint signings with my longtime critique pal, Beth Terrell-Hicks, who later shortened her by-line to Beth Terrell, then Jaden Terrell. We shared a tent or a booth at many events for several years. She also became my chief editor on future books from Night Shadows Press. November brought an end to NSP's relationship with Wingspan Press when Ben and I realized we were buying books from Wingspan who bought them from

Lightning Source, the publishing arm of Ingram Books, located just down the road from Nashville in La Vergne. We set up an account with Lightning Source and began dealing directly with them. It not only cut out the middleman but saved me on shipping costs.

Much of *The Marathon Murders* took place in Trousdale County, one of the state's smallest, to the northeast of Nashville. It had only one city, Hartsville, which served as the county seat. That brought the Tennessee Bureau of Investigation into the picture since the local cops had little experience with murders. I had visited TBI Headquarters and toured the whole operation. Sarah and I traveled up to Hartsville in January of 2009 where I spoke to the Trousdale County Historical Society. Those in attendance asked lots of interesting questions, and we sold a few books.

I had completed writing the first Sid Chance book back in 2007 and sent out a bunch of agent queries, which went nowhere as usual. Readers have always liked my books, but agents never seemed to want to take a chance on me. This round of queries took place during the shakeup with Durban House and the short arrangement with Wingspan. I had dropped the project until I got *Marathon* well on the road. Working directly with Lightning Source, I had the new book, *The Surest Poison*, ready to go in April 2009. Since my earlier books had been well received at my church, I scheduled the book launch for a Saturday afternoon at City Road Chapel United Methodist Church in Madison. Here's the plot blurb:

Three seemingly unrelated murders crop up during the investigation of a decade-old chemical dump that plagues a rural community west of Nashville. PI Sid Chance, a former National Parks ranger whose career as a small town police chief was cut short by malicious accusations of bribery, pursues the case after being coaxed out of self-imposed exile by Jaz LeMieux, a wealthy ex-cop. Is the man responsible for the pollution dead or alive? Who is having Sid tailed and threatened? When Jaz helps with the investigation, she is awakened by an explosion behind her mansion. Is it related to the abduction of her retainers' grandson, or Sid's case? As the tension mounts, Sid finds himself confronting the unsavory people responsible for his past troubles.

Jaz is one of my favorite characters, and I received lots of comments on her from readers. During our travels up north and out west we stopped many times at Pilot truck stops, or Flying J, for gas and/or cappuccino, a drink to which we became addicted. Having spent a lot of time in Knoxville, I knew about the Haslam family and the Pilot company. This was before they bought Flying J and before Bill Haslam became governor of Tennessee. At any rate, I used the idea for Jaz's background. She inherited a chain of truck stops when her father died. The genesis of the book came from a chat I had at a high school alumni luncheon, a monthly event known as the East High Lunch Bunch. Another East alum, Norma Mott Tillman, worked as a PI who specialized in finding missing persons. She told me about a case she had handled in Jackson, Tennessee involving a trichloroethylene spill found on her client's property. The state had come after him to pay for the cleanup. It had been there when he bought the property, but the previous owner could not be found. She had to track down the guilty party. I moved it to a small county just west of Nashville and threw a few murders into the mix. I stewed around a bit for a title and finally read a quote from Ralph Waldo Emerson who wrote "the surest poison is time." It fit perfectly with the story.

I had turned back to Greg McKenzie for book five in the series and kept working on the new plot. Set around Nashville in the Christmas season, it required research regarding the professional sports angle. We made a few out-of-town events and at least a couple of signings a month during the rest of 2009. Grandson Justin Jones entered a private school that fall, and we had more school-related programs to keep up with. We bought him a drum and he played in the school band. The week before Christmas, we took him and his cousin, Dalton Pursley, to see a Christmas show in Branson, Missouri.

Justin joined an Upward Basketball team in January, and we cheered from the sidelines at least once a week, usually more. The season ran through the first of March. We stayed fairly close to home during the first half of the year, traveling no farther north than Bowling Green, Kentucky (Southern Kentucky BookFest) and south to Belle Buckle, Tennessee (RC-Moon Pie Festival). Justin began taking Taekwondo lessons during the summer and also joined the Boy Scouts. We spent a lot of time keeping up with him. By the end of the summer I had *A Sporting Murder* ready for Lightning Source. On September 25th the book launch party took place at Mysteries & More book store (now, unfortunately, closed) in Lenox Village, on the south side of Nashville. Here's the plot blurb:

Goodwill to men isn't the Yuletide theme when Greg and Jill McKenzie are hired to investigate rumors that something shady is involved in a deal to bring an NBA basketball team to Nashville. Their client is attorney for a group of Nashville Predators NHL hockey fans who don't think there's room for both pro hockey and pro basketball. When Greg goes to meet an informant, he finds the young man shot to death. What information did he have that would "blow your mind?" Things turn deadlier when a bomb goes off beneath Greg's Jeep. Complicating matters, a disgruntled felon Greg helped send to prison during his Air Force OSI career shows up with revenge in mind. The explosive situation reaches a climax on Christmas Day.

Although I finished with the writing in 2010, to keep the continuity of the series, the story took place in 2004. This resulted in a little juggling of the facts. In 2004 the Predators, Nashville's NHL hockey team, played in what was called the Gaylord Entertainment Center. By the time of the writing it had become the Bridgestone Arena, which it still is. As a result, I referred to it simply as "the arena." Another shift had taken place in the police department, as I realized when I took part in a Citizen's Police Academy. I had done a ride-along with a Metro detective back around the period depicted in the book, and the Homicide Division worked out of the Criminal Justice Center downtown. But I learned that a few years later, homicide detectives had been spread out among the precincts. I kept them where they were in 2004.

I had a list of people to thank in the acknowledgements, including Justin's Taekwondo instructor, Louie Aregis. When he found out I was a mystery writer, he wanted to be a character in my next book. A bad guy. If you read *A Sporting Murder*, you'll find that is indeed what he became. I also thanked Michael Bunch, a member of my Sisters in Crime chapter. The story involved an arson problem, and I discovered that Mike was a certified arson investigator with the Nashville Fire Department. One intriguing comment on the page said: "A source who prefers to remain anonymous gave me some valuable insights into the background of the local criminal element." Unfortunately, I've forgotten the source's identity. With six books in my inventory now, I did quite a few signings in the next several weeks, including at the Southern Festival of Books in Nashville, the Kentucky Book Fair in Lexington, and a special event in Louisville, Kentucky.

We did a few signings around the area during the winter in 2011. In March we headed back to the Flora-Bama area, referring to the two states although the name belongs to a well-known lounge at the state line on Perdido Key Drive. Signings in the area included our favorite Pensacola library and Barnes & Noble at Spanish Fort. In April I began attending the Metro Nashville Citizens Police Academy, which met for three hours on eight consecutive Tuesday nights. They have expanded it now to twelve weeks. I found it an ideal experience for a mystery writer. We listened to officers from the various specialized sections of the department describe what they did. One night a sergeant parked his squad car in front of the building and showed us all the radio equipment they use. On another occasion we went to the police firing range, and we visited the communications center where they answered 911 calls.

Early in May I took part in the Honor Flight program. I was one of around 100 World War II veterans from the Nashville area who were flown to Washington, D.C. to visit the World War II Memorial, among other sites. Southwest Airlines provided the round-trip flight at no cost to the veterans. We left the bus on our way back to the airport to spend some time at the Air Force Memorial with its three soaring spires. I enjoyed that.

Between all the events taking place I had been working on another book, which would be the second in the Sid Chance Series. I bucked the convention that short titles are best and named it *The Good, The Bad and The Murderous*. I also went against my better judgment and designed the cover myself. It featured a black silhouette of a standing man with outstretched arm holding a pistol. The background is solid red with the title and a small blurb reversed out in white. I finished work on the book in early August and sent it to the printer. Here's the blurb:

Medicare fraud, drug trafficking, a hired killer, a crooked cop, it's a nightmare scenario PI Sid Chance finds himself in when he takes a tough assignment— prove a young man just out of prison for a murder when he was twelve did not commit a new homicide. Everything is thrown upside down when Jaz LeMieux, the wealthy ex-cop working with him on the case, finds herself accused of a despicable crime, and the evidence is damning. When a hit man comes after Sid, all hell breaks loose.

Also in August, Sarah and I volunteered to take over the seniors group at church, which entailed planning and directing monthly trips to various sites in the local area and far beyond. We also did occasional signings, and in September we attended the inaugural session of the Writers Police Academy in Greensboro, North Carolina. Run by ex-cop Lee Lofland, it offered a schedule of sessions that provided an array of information valuable to mystery writers. Lofland also wrote a blog titled "The Graveyard Shift" on subjects of interest to writers. A month after the release of *The Good, The Bad and The Murderous*, another former Durban House author joined our ranks at Night Shadows Press. We released Mark W. Danielson's first Maxx Watts Mystery, *Writer's Block*.

January 2012 began with a library signing in Manchester, some 70 miles south of Nashville. That was followed the next week with cataract surgery on one eye, two weeks later the other eye. After that I tossed away my glasses, something I had worn since my newspaper days in Knoxville, many, many years ago. It seemed almost miraculous. I did have one problem with the second eye surgery. The doctor did not put me to sleep totally as she needed to give me some instructions, but after it was over, she advised that my heart rate dropped to 40 and they had to take measures get it back up. We headed out to a couple of book festivals in April, and did two other signings in June.

I went downtown to Sandy Campbell's photography studio in July to have photos made for the back cover of new books, as well as for my website. The old one had gotten a bit out of date. Though no relation, Sandy (real name Frank Sanford) had grown up a few blocks from my house in Madison. His dad, Spiller Campbell, had been in my Sunday School class for years. A precise man who chose his words with care, Spiller practiced law and served as Probate Court Master. A short, unassuming man, you'd never guess that he had flown nightfighters in Sicily and Southern France during World War II, then flew F-94 Starfire jet fighters out of Alaska during the Korean War.

After finishing with *The Good, The Bad and The Murderous*, I checked the pile of manuscripts on my office floor and decided to take another look at those first three I had completed in the early nineties. Starting with *Beware the Jabberwock*, I read the manuscript and the comments from editors. Along with the editors, I liked the story, but it needed a bit of revision. I put it up first as an ebook on Amazon and Smashwords in the spring of 2012. Along the way I looked into Amazon's publishing arm, CreateSpace. In contrast to Lightning Source, they charged no setup fee. The drawback involved distribution. They required using CreateSpace as the publisher to get distribution to bookstores and libraries. I wanted my books published by Night Shadows Press, and that's what I got. All I wanted was books to sell at signings. By the end of July, I received a box full of *Beware the Jabberwock* from CreateSpace. I added them to my display at events like Gallatin's Main Street Festival, the Southern Festival of Books, Killer Nashville, and a Holiday Bazaar at Church.

January of 2013 got the year off to a mixed bag of a start. First, Sarah had surgery to implant a pacemaker. She had been diagnosed with a heart arrhythmia, and the cardiologist said a pacemaker would correct it. Shortly after that I drove down to Manchester to sign books at a library event which went quite well. In March I spoke to the Stones River Woman's Club at Marathon Village. We met in the old show room, and the ladies bought lots of copies of *The Marathon Murders*. We headed out of town in April to attend Derek Pacifico's Writer's Homicide School in Knoxville. A retired sergeant in the San Bernardino County Sheriff's Department, he had several year's experience as a homicide detective. He has since come out of retirement to serve as chief of police in Harriman, Tennessee. We did a repeat performance at the RC-Moon Pie Festival in June and at Killer Nashville in August. I had been working on revisions of the second book in what I labeled the Post Cold War Political Thriller Trilogy. I sent the new version of *The Poksu Conspiracy* to CreateSpace and had books in hand by the end of June. It became my largest paperback at 524 pages.

September brought a grand plan, a full week at a resort near Tampa, Florida. But for me, grand plans have a way of turning into grand disasters. On the way, we spent the night at a motel in Dothan, Alabama, which I figured was approximately the halfway point. I woke sometime after midnight and went to the bathroom. They had put us in a handicapped room and the bathroom floor was solid tile with a shower in the corner. When I didn't come back to bed, Sarah came to check and found me stretched out on my back, blood oozing out on the tile behind my head. She called 911, and they hauled me off to a nearby hospital. I fully recovered consciousness in about half an hour on the examination table. They kept me overnight, and then Sarah's daughter, Judy Metcalf, came down to drive us home. As had happened several times in the past twenty or so years, after similar falls but none so hard on my noggin, they examined me thoroughly and found nothing physically wrong. During the rest of 2013 I did a few more signings, but nothing nearly as exciting took place.

I finished work on the last of the Post Cold War Political Thriller Trilogy books, *Overture to Disaster*, shortly after *Poksu* came out, and for some reason, perhaps because of running low on cash, decided to make it strictly an ebook. It appeared on Amazon for the Kindle at the end of August 2013. Another lengthy novel, *Overture* shifts from the Ukraine to Washington, from a special operations mission in Iran to a courts-martial in Florida, and from the Belarus capital to Mexico and back to Washington. Around this time, Night Shadows Press published Mark Danielson's second Maxx Watts mystery, *Spectral Gallows*.

In November I hit the 88 mark, and in February of 2014 Sarah made it to 81. That was the month my older brother Jim died after going downhill for several months. He was happy after having made it past 90. That was also the last time I heard from my "little" brother, Howard. He's taller than me, but eleven years younger. He spent quite a few years running businesses in Saudi Arabia and along the way married a nurse there from Australia. He sold out his interests in Saudi and left just before the Arab uprisings in 2010. They resettled near her folks. When I called him about Jim, he said he couldn't come to the funeral, but he'd come to the States that summer. If he did, he forgot to tell us.

Sarah and I slowed considerably on our travel, except to doctors' offices. As we would tell friends, our social life mainly involved trips to the doctor. In April, she followed me to the day surgery suite to get her cataracts removed. And in May I decided it was time to do something about my deteriorating voice. I had become reluctant to take on speaking engagements because of the inability to project above a normal voice. I went back to see Dr. Robert Ossoff, head of the Vanderbilt Voice Center, where most of the country singers with voice problems went for treatment. Their pictures appeared all over the walls in waiting rooms inside the clinic. I had first seen Dr. Ossoff back in 2003 and had benefited from his advice, though when I asked if I'd be a successful country singer when he finished, his answer was, "I don't think so." At any rate, things were getting worse now. He doubled a medication I had been taking and set me up for voice therapy sessions.

For several months Sarah had talked about her frustration with the steps at home. Having to navigate a flight of stairs from the garage to the kitchen, as well as walking up a succession of steps to get to the front door, had proved quite taxing. And a trip to the mailbox meant walking farther downhill on the driveway. In late spring we decided to move to a place that sat flat on the ground, with fewer rooms to take care of. That necessitated getting rid of tons of "stuff." First we checked with Sarah's clan, then mine, to see who wanted what. After that we started gathering the rest of the stuff we didn't need for a sale. We did quite well with what we called a moving sale at the end of June. My daughters came in from Oak Ridge and Decatur, Georgia to help. As it developed, we did too well, selling several tools I've had to replace.

With that out of the way, we contacted a real estate agent and told him what we wanted to do. He and his assistant showed our house and quickly found a buyer. Next he drove us to the opposite end (southwest tip) of Nashville, in the Bellevue suburb. He chose a development called River Plantation that featured condominiums on both sides of Sawyer Brown Road stretching for more than a mile. They were built over a number of years starting with Section I (Roman numeral 1) just off Highway 70-S. We looked first at a few units in Section XI. They appeared nice but were expensive, and we didn't feel particularly impressed. He took us down the hill to Section X and approached a vacant unit through the carport. We entered the living room and faced a hallway leading to the front door. Once we looked out the front, we were virtually hooked. Instead of facing a busy street or another condo, as with the other places we had seen, this one had a brief front yard past a sidewalk where the terrain dropped off precipitously to a strip of grassland, then a short clump of trees, and beyond that the scenic Harpeth River. The price was considerably better than the others we had looked at, plus the owner agreed to cut it by $5,000 if we would take care of a few problems like repainting the walls and replacing the dishwasher. We agreed and spent a lot less than $5,000 on fix-up. A week after attending the Killer Nashville Conference, we closed on the property and moved in.

During the rest of the year I worked on a revision of another manuscript I had originally sent to Bob Thixton at Jay Garon-Brooke, *Hell Bound*. We also continued to do several more signings, including the Gallatin Main Street Festival and McGavock High School Christmas Craft Fair. In addition we did a couple of events not far from our new home at Bellevue's Red Caboose Park.

In January of 2015, exactly two years after Sarah got her pacemaker, I had one added to my chest. While the agents were showing our house the previous August, I had pulled my passing out routine again and knocked a hole in the bathroom wall with my elbow. It didn't hurt me, and I was only unconscious briefly. But my Dalton, Georgia episode had been only eleven months before. I consulted a cardiologist, and he eventually sent me to the same surgeon who had inserted Sarah's pacemaker. The surgeon assured me it would keep my heart rate from slowing to the point where I could lose consciousness. It involved inserting the little battery-operated device just below the collarbone on the left side. A thin wire connected the pacemaker to my heart. Later in the month we did a multi-author signing event at the new Bellevue branch library. At the end of February, Sarah and I made a trek up I-24 to Metropolis, Illinois, a journey we had made countless times before to Harrah's Casino. I don't remember how we made out that time, but we never won or lost more than a few hundred dollars. We didn't go to sporting events or concerts and we didn't eat out much. We looked at playing the slots as our recreation. I mention this trip because it appeared it might be our last solo flight. Shortly after this, Sarah and her daughter decided since my ninetieth birthday would be coming up later that year, I should no longer be driving long distances. The Nashville area, okay. I thought it rather silly but went along since we hadn't talked about making any long trips anyway.

Around this time I finished work on the book I

renamed *Hellbound*, one word instead of two, and sent it to Lightning Source. On reflection, it became the most personal account of anything I had written. Almost biographical in some respects, it featured a character who lived on Gartland Avenue in a house similar to the one in which I grew up at 1300 Gartland. She attended East Nashville High School in the early years of World War II, as I did. She graduated from the University of Tennessee and moved to Madison after marriage. But the most personal part of the story concerned the bus trip to New Orleans. It mirrored in every detail the tour Sarah and I took with the church group from Madison back in the middle nineties, before we married. Up until the appearance of a hurricane. Fortunately, we didn't have that problem. Here's the blurb I used on the book:

When a busload of seniors from a suburban Nashville church heads down the Natchez Trace on a carefree journey to The Big Easy, they are unaware that a Mafia hit squad is playing a deadly game of tag with them. All except one passenger. The man they know as Bryce Reynolds is really Pat Pagano, a successful Las Vegas stockbroker who was lured into handling investments for a New York crime family. After his two grown sons are killed in an attack by a rival gang and his wife succumbs to cancer, Pagano decimates the mob with his testimony in federal court. He disappears, then resurfaces in Nashville as Reynolds, a retired businessman from Oklahoma. But after years of searching, an old Mafia enforcer tracks Pagano to the church bus en route to New Orleans.

I mentioned earlier the decision to curtail my driving activities. When daughters Anne and Betsy and I decided to visit son Mark in Florida a few months later, Betsy drove down from Oak Ridge to pick us up on the way to

Pensacola. In August when my last single Campbell grandson, Ed, and his bride-to-be scheduled their wedding for Pigeon Forge in the Smoky Mountains, Anne drove from Georgia to pick us up on the way. Judy, Sarah's daughter, drove us to Metropolis later in the year for "recreation" at Harrah's. Because of her job, she could only go on weekends, which meant Saturdays. But the freebies we got in the mail each month were only good Sunday through Thursday. In the spring of 2016, we decided to go during the week, using our free night at the hotel, and tell Judy after we returned. May brought a question in my mind about the effectiveness of the decision to implant a pacemaker in my chest. One night I used the small bathroom down the hallway in the wee hours, then started back to the bedroom. The next thing I knew, I lay in the hallway with Sarah frantically calling me. I had passed out again despite the pacemaker. Sarah's son, Bill, was there at the time, and he drove us to the Emergency Room a little later. They examined me and, as usual, found nothing obviously wrong. The ER doctor diagnosed it as "syncope," which the dictionary defines as "a brief loss of consciousness caused by a temporary deficiency of oxygen in the brain." A slowed heart rate could cause that, but my pacemaker wouldn't permit it to drop below 60 beats per minute. Sounded like the problem I've had for years. Source unknown.

After we moved to Bellevue, we found a Methodist church only a few blocks from our condo. We transferred our membership to Bellevue United Methodist Church, and in August of 2016 I began work as a member of the Archives Committee. At City Road Chapel in Madison, as I mentioned earlier, the archives consisted of a few books and a bunch of manila folders stuffed with papers of historical interest that resided in a metal filing cabinet, plus a few assorted documents that dealt with the past century and a half. Bellevue UMC, over 200 years old, had been blessed with a professional archivist as a member. The wife of a retired minister, Margaret Cornell had organized the church's historic documents in some ninety professional archival boxes stacked on shelves that covered one wall of the Archives Room. We worked each Tuesday afternoon that month. I began with sorting a box of audio tapes containing sermons from several years back. Some of the ladies worked with board and committee minutes.

The remainder of 2016 proved unremarkable, although I did provide the program for the Sisters in Crime chapter one month by sitting up front and answering questions about my writing life. I had explained to my buddy Beth Terrell, who had succeeded me as president, that my voice wouldn't hold out for a talk, but I could answer questions.

I continued to see Dr. Ossoff at the Vanderbilt Voice Center, and he put me on a bunch of Gabapentin pills, which were normally used for patients with seizures. They had found it helped with coughs because it deadened the feelings of the vocal chords, as I understood it. Sometimes the throat got tricked into thinking the vocal chords were foreign bodies which needed to be coughed up. It helped some, but I still experienced occasional coughing sprees that left me barely able to speak.

The year 2017 brought a new problem having to do with my short term memory, particularly in respect to things like coming up with specific words, such as names of people I had associated with for years, and places or products I know as well as my own name. I conveniently ascribed the problem to all the Gabapentin pills, though it as likely could be attributed to advancing age (sounds better than "old age"). This period also marked the beginning of my work on this tome. Perhaps I shouldn't be using that term, however. My *Webster's Collegiate* defines "tome" as a book, especially a large or scholarly one.

Before completing this project it might be fruitful to take stock of what Sarah and I have helped contribute to the ranks of homo sapiens. As mentioned earlier, Alma and I had two sons and two daughters. The oldest, Steve, has two sons–Dan and his wife, Laura, have three daughters; Andrew and his wife, Mindy, have one son. Number two son Mark also has two sons–John and his wife, Kristen, have three boys and expecting another; Ed and his new wife, Michelle, have no children, yet. Older daughter Anne is unmarried. The youngest, Betsy, and her husband, Jim, have two daughters and two sons, Wendy, Melody, Harry, and Jeremy, none married, two still being educated, one in high school, one in college. That's four children, eight grandchildren, and seven great-grandchildren. Adding in Sarah's family gives two more children, Judy and Bill; three grandchildren, Tina, Brandy, and Justin; and five great-grandchildren. Between the two of us, we've added 29 to the population count, of which we are justifiably proud.

It is now near the end of the summer of 2017, and as my personal tale winds down, I look back on the past 91 and-a-half years with a bit of nostalgia. There were things I would do differently in retrospect, and there are things I would still like to do but won't likely have the opportunity. Overall, though, I would paraphrase the title of the old Jimmy Stewart movie that shows up every Christmas and say it's been a wonderful life. I've been a lot of places and done a lot of things, and most of it I've thoroughly enjoyed.

Maybe at 101 I'll write a post script.

The following is an excerpt from my latest book, a suspense novel titled *Hellbound*.
The first book outside my three series, it introduces a completely new cast of characters. As mentioned in my memoir, it is the most personal of my fiction writing.

October 1999
Nashville, Tennessee

1

Moving like a hurricane ready for landfall, slow, deliberate, destruction on his mind, Boots Minelli paused at the door. With that innate sense of the totally committed, he felt the payoff almost within his grasp. After years of chasing down false trails and blundering up blind alleys, he would soon see the terror in the traitor's eyes. The bastard who had nearly wrecked the Vicario "family" no longer had his days numbered. It was now only a matter of hours.

The thin metal pick looked like a toothpick in his beefy hands, and though he hadn't used the gadget in years, Boots wielded the thin metal pick with the ease of a locksmith. Pulling the heavy, wood-paneled door open, he squeezed through. Not that the doorway was any narrower than normal, but Boots had the size and demeanor of a snorting bull.

In his black outfit, he could have passed for an undertaker, which wasn't that far off the mark. He lingered in the slate-floored foyer, stared into the living room, noted the faint lemony odor of a cleaning spray. It led him to suspect the room's tidy, vacuumed appearance was the result of a housekeeper's recent visit. The only thing out of place was a folded piece of paper on the floor.

The effort of stooping to pick it up left him panting, mouth agape, like some dumb-ass hound he might have

The effort of stooping to pick it up left him panting, mouth agape, like some dumb-ass hound he might have chased off to fetch a stick. Ridiculous, he thought. Maddening. But that was the way a lousy fate had treated him lately. A big man in his middle fifties with abundant black hair, he had a bloated face, a joyless twist to his thick, pursed lips, and a body that made him a prime candidate for by-pass surgery.

Boots unfolded the paper and tilted it toward the light from he window. A heading identified the sheet as the itinerary for Lovely Lane United Methodist Church's "LLSS New Orleans Tour."

Beneath that was a list of dates and times for the week, starting with Monday:

"7:30 a.m. Board Bus, Depart Lovely Lane."

"1:00 p.m. Lunch at Barnes Crossing, Tupelo, MS."

"2:00 p.m. On to Natchez, MS, to spend the night."

The gold Rolex on Boots' massive wrist showed not quite seven a.m. A little earlier, parked in his rental car a short distance up the quiet suburban street from the red brick ranch, he had watched the man who called himself Bryce Reynolds pull out of the driveway in a four-year-old charcoal gray Buick. If Reynolds was leaving on the church bus at 7:30, Boots had a detailed schedule of where the man could be intercepted along the way to or from New Orleans.

But Boots had worked too hard and too long to risk any slip-ups. He needed a positive ID. Shoving the paper into his pocket, he launched a quick search of the house. Three-bedrooms, two-and-a-half-baths. One of the bedrooms had been furnished as an office. He pulled on a pair of sterile gloves and began to probe about the desk with surgical precision. He found a few utility bills, brochures promoting investment newsletters, an ad for a music CD club. Mostly he spotted Post-It notes stuck everywhere. It resembled a mini-billboard jungle—reminders of bills to pay, events coming up, checklists of things to do. One note confirmed Reynolds' plans to be on the New Orleans bus tour. *He's in his seventies*, Boots thought, *tends to forget things if they aren't written down.*

Though certain Reynolds was not the man's real name, Boots found nothing around the desk that would hint at a concealed identity. Next he turned to the family room. He found strictly masculine furniture, heavy wooden pieces informally placed. But he had an odd feeling that something was missing. Then it hit him.

No pictures. Not a single photograph was displayed anywhere in the house, the mark of a man with a hidden past.

As he shifted his gaze about the wood-paneled room, Boots thought of the years of searching that had finally paid off. He finally had a current name and address for the man whose testimony at the big New York Mafia trial in the early nineties had decimated the Vicario stronghold.

Though there were no photographs, Boots noticed the walls had been decorated with paintings. They included a tranquil mountain village draped in snow, a melancholy lighthouse beside foaming breakers, a drab old grist mill amidst a fiery display of fall foliage. Boots had no taste for art, but he guessed these were valuable paintings, not knockoffs turned out in some assembly line operation. The traitor had money. He could afford the real thing.

Boots stared at the grist mill, but his thoughts strayed to the contact he had employed in Tennessee to dig into Reynolds' background. There was little to be found. The man kept to himself, made no close friendships. He had bought the house in Madison, an unincorporated suburb on the northeastern side of Metropolitan Nashville, in 1995. His only slip had been a mention that he came from Tulsa.

A check in Tulsa turned up records of a Bryce Reynolds who had gone bankrupt in 1992. He started drinking heavily, and his wife left him. He disappeared from the radar screens shortly afterward. Presently he would have been in his early sixties, but Boots' source said the Madison Reynolds was likely over seventy.

The bright colors of the leaves around the grist mill slowly dragged Boots' attention back to the painting. Then he had an idea. He walked over and pulled the frame away from the wall enough to peek in back. Nothing. He checked the lighthouse, in a smaller, vertical frame. This try rewarded him with the outline of a cutout panel.

The thump of excitement in his chest triggered a brief return of breathlessness. Boots took a moment to catch his breath then removed the painting from the wall. He pried the panel open with a pocket knife, revealing the combination lock of a wall safe. Probably an old one, he thought, put in when the house was built back in the sixties. A simple "box job." Safecracking was a skill he had learned from a fellow student during his happily brief sojourn at a New York facility for the education of the criminally inclined, otherwise known as the state prison at Attica.

He flattened a large ear against the safe and gingerly twisted the dial. In the silence of the room, he listened to the soft click as the tumblers landed in position. He had the door open quickly. Inside lay a stack of "C notes," crisp hundred-dollar-bills bound with rubber bands, likely a few thousand bucks. The safe also contained a handgun, but what caught his eye was a photograph and a long, thin case. He checked the picture first.

Bingo! A man and a woman, with two smiling younger men. He immediately recognized Patrick Pagano, his wife, Ellen, and their sons, Paul and Phillip. He knew what was in the case before he had it open. A star-shaped medallion with the word VALOR beneath an eagle's outstretched wings, attached to a blue ribbon emblazoned with white stars. On the back was engraved "Sgt. Patrick O. Pagano, December 22, 1944, Bastogne, Belgium."

The Congressional Medal of Honor. A flag-waving patriot despite his problems with the government, Tony Vicario had proudly bragged about having a Medal of Honor winner on his payroll.

Boots mustered the first genuine smile he had allowed himself in ages. He had withheld details of Pagano's new identity from his boss until he could be certain he had the right man. Now he would tell Vicario he had accomplished the seemingly impossible.

2

THE CHURCH parking lot had not seen so much activity this early on a Monday morning since a visitor tossed a burning cigarette into a trash can, starting a mini-conflagration that turned a nearby fence into charcoal. In addition to cars pulling up to liberate hopping, skipping, squealing youngsters headed for the Lovely Lane Day Care Center, others dropped off an equally excited, though less demonstrative, group of folks at the other end of the time spectrum. They tugged and dragged stuffed travel bags over to a big red and white bus with Nova Tours painted on the sides, highlighted by a stylized shooting star logo.

The bus blocked one lane of the parking lot beside the impressive stone building, its diesel engine rumbling impatiently. Not half as impatient, though, as the tall, thin woman who lingered beside the open door. Her angular face, accented by wide green eyes that kept searching for someone, was topped by a shock of frilly gray hair that overhung her brow like tendrils of Spanish moss. Her glasses, encased in thin metal frames, had been tilted up and jammed into her hair. At sixty-nine, Matilda Ellis was a marvel of movement, a highly charged bundle of energy.

"If forty-three other people can get here by seven-thirty," she said in the deep voice that rang from the alto section of the choir on Sunday mornings, "you'd think Sadie Blevins could, too."

"Want me to go in and call her, Tillie?" asked a short, dumpy woman standing nearby. "Surely she didn't forget."

Tillie Ellis gave a deep sigh. "Don't bet on it. That woman would forget her name if it wasn't printed on her Social Security card. Go ahead and call, Polly. If she's still there, tell her we're about to send the sheriff after her."

The tardy passenger represented only a minor annoyance. The real source of Tillie's frown lay on page five of the morning newspaper stuffed among her belongings on the front seat. A story that ran barely five paragraphs, the item chronicled a tropical storm that had just reached hurricane status in the West Indies. A retired travel agent, Tillie had listened with growing anxiety on numerous occasions to a colleague's harrowing tale of being trapped in Miami by Hurricane Andrew seven years ago. The possibility of a similar fate had plagued Tillie during hurricane seasons ever since, a hangover from a fear of storms acquired when she was still in pigtails. The prospect concerned her even more now, with all the time and effort she had invested in this trip.

She turned to the driver, a stocky black man with thinning salt-and-pepper hair, dressed to match his bus in white shirt, dark red pants and tie. "Have you ever been on a bus caught in a hurricane, Chick?"

Chick Townes leaned against the door and shook his head. "No, ma'am. What's more, I got no desire to."

"Well, let's pray it doesn't happen this time." She glanced over at the church. "It looks like we may have a little delay, though, waiting for Sadie Blevins. That any problem?"

"Not unless the weather really turns ugly on us," he said. "If we get away by eight o'clock, we ought to be in pretty good shape."

Most of the passengers were already in their seats,

dressed in a variety of casual outfits, some topped off with sweaters or light jackets. That would change the farther south they went. A few of the men were out strolling around the parking lot. Tillie stepped down to the asphalt and encountered Polly Pitts waddling up like a small, plump duck.

"Sadie said she was just going out the door," Polly said. "Claimed she'd be here within fifteen minutes."

"Thanks." Tillie shrugged off a twinge of remorse. "I guess I shouldn't talk about her. I'll probably be worse than that when I'm eighty." *And I may feel like eighty a lot sooner if that hurricane doesn't stay down in the tropics where it belongs*, she mused.

A RETIREE from the DuPont plant across the Cumberland River in Old Hickory, Fred Scott kept pace with his casually dressed companion as they strolled past the bus toward the street, where a changing traffic light brought a wail of screeching tires. He tried to think of something that might get Bryce Reynolds talking. "Looks like old Tillie's really keyed up this morning," he said. "Bet she spent half the night getting everything ready."

"Yeah," Bryce said. His face showed no trace of what he thought about it. "Putting this together must have been a monstrous job."

"You ever done one of these bus trips before?"

"No."

"Guess you were too busy making a living."

Neither his voice nor his expression changed as Bryce replied. "Guess so."

They walked along in silence, Fred adjusting his John Deere cap and puzzling over how to do a better job of pulling his new friend out of that hard shell he'd erected around himself. Fred knew he'd made a little progress, recalling Tillie's telephone conversation a few weeks back after he had suggested she call Bryce about this trip. Fred had listened in on an extension in the church office. After introducing herself, Tillie launched into a persuasive sales pitch.

"Fred Scott suggested I call you about our Lovely Lane Silver Shadows trip to New Orleans. It will be six days in October, a real fun-filled adventure. Are you familiar with our Silver Shadows group?"

"Senior citizens, isn't it?" Bryce asked.

Tillie had glanced at Fred and waved a hand. "I'd say we were more than just a senior citizens group. Anyway, I think most of us prefer to be known by the more genteel term mature adults."

"I don't think I've ever been with a group of mature adults," Bryce said, a hint of humor in his voice. "I'm not sure I would fit in."

"Of course you would. Fred has told me all about you."

Fred groaned. That "all" was actually quite limited. Bryce said little about himself.

Tillie charged on. "I think you'd find the group very convivial. We have lots of single ladies signing up for the trip. Actually, most are widows. The males are just about all accompanying wives."

"So I would be the token bachelor? I'm really a widower, you know. My wife died several years ago."

"I'm sure you won't be the only one," she said.

In the end, she had talked him into signing up for the trip.

When Fred and Bryce reached the sidewalk that bordered the church parking lot, they turned toward a black asphalt apron surrounding a drugstore that stood adjacent to the church property. As they strolled along,

Bryce caught the cheerful sound of a solitary mockingbird serenading them from a nearby oak tree.

"I heard a new joke yesterday," Fred said, glancing around. He caught a flash of the odd twist Bryce's straight slash of a mouth showed with the telling of a funny story, one of the few emotions he had coaxed out of the man.

"This another farmer tale?" Bryce asked, his wide brown eyes beginning to shine.

"I'm really just a farmer at heart, you know." Fred lived on a small farm down in Neely's Bend, a part of Madison formed by one of numerous serpentine twists the Cumberland River took while meandering through Nashville. The area was an anachronism, a small chunk of rural America plunked down in the midst of a heavily populated suburb of Metropolitan Nashville.

"Okay, let's have it," Bryce said.

"Seems this farmer called the vet about a problem with a cantankerous bull that kept breaking out of the pen, giving the heifers a hard time. The vet says, 'I thought I sent you some pills to keep that bull from getting so excited.' 'You did,' the farmer replied. 'But I had to throw 'em away.' 'Why on earth?' asked the vet. The farmer said, 'Because my wife found out what they were for and I was afraid she'd put 'em in my coffee.'"

Bryce shook his head as he laughed. "Fred, you've got more stories than McDonald's has hamburgers."

THEY WERE halfway down the lot when something odd caught Bryce's eye over near the drugstore. He stopped abruptly and stared at a tan car with the driver-side door open. A leg protruded from it. The rest of the man's body appeared to be leaning the other way.

"That guy looks like he's in trouble," Bryce said. He ran toward the car.

Fred jogged behind him.

As they approached the vehicle, Bryce saw an expensive-looking cowboy boot stuck out the door like a large leather exclamation point. The man appeared monstrous in size. He clutched one hand to his throat.

"Are you all right?" Bryce called out.

As he leaned into the car, a shock wave froze him into numbness. He stared at the flushed face of Boots Minelli, one of the most feared capos in the Vicario crime family.

3

ON LEAVING Pagano/Reynolds' house, Boots had decided to go by the church and check on the bus. He remembered passing the rambling stone structure on the way in and knew he would have no trouble finding it. Afterward, he would contact his young sidekick, Dominick Locasio, and the three other "wise guys" who had accompanied him to Nashville. They would rendezvous at the car rental agency before heading south.

Elated at what he had found after all those years of fruitless searching, Boots drove with a semblance of a smile, a decided change from his normal dour expression during those difficult times. He had never remotely considered giving up, of course. He was the most loyal and devoted subordinate of the The Boss, Anthony Vicario, who had chosen Boots as a young stalwart to enforce one of Tony's main credos, "death to traitors." Let a turncoat get away and it would spread like an infectious disease.

Rush hour traffic was building as Boots pulled onto Gallatin Road, the main drag through this northern suburb. A mish-mash of fast food outlets, cloned service stations, small retailers, and a few chain stores crowded each other for exposure along the busy strip. He had seen enough of Nashville. He hated country music, and he was sick of hearing about the Tennessee Titans. Thank God he'd be leaving shortly. According to the itinerary in his pocket, the bus would travel down the Natchez Trace

Parkway, with the group scheduled to spend the night at a Days Inn in Natchez.

That would be the place to take care of business, he thought. A call to his room would lure Reynolds out. They would whisk him off to some secluded spot where he would have the opportunity to sweat over his misdeeds, then Boots would ventilate the bastard's head with 9mm slugs. In his view, it was a simple business proposition, a permanent solution to an annoying problem. It made him quite a different breed, or so he reasoned, from such ogres as serial killer Jeffrey Dahmer or mass murderers like Charles Manson. Boots looked forward to making his report back to The Boss that Pagano had ceased to exist.

As he drove along, dodging the zany Nashville drivers, Boots saw a couple of boys jostling each other as they waited for a school bus and recalled his own life as a youngster in Brooklyn. Monstrous in size even then, he had liked nothing better than making things miserable for other young punks. Though not well-educated in a formal sense, he had the equivalent of an advanced degree in street smarts. He graduated from petty larceny to armed robbery, then joined the outfit as a "soldier" in a group involved in loan sharking. He loved to knock heads when some poor slob got behind in his payments.

In the 1980s he was made a capodecina, captain of his own crew involved in mob activities. He escaped the trials brought on by Pagano as he was on an overseas sojourn back in the old country, recovering from a shooting injury. He hid out for three years, then returned after the heat had subsided. Intensely loyal to Tony Vicario, he happily took on the mission of tracking down the traitor who had tried to destroy the family.

When he arrived at the church, Boots saw the bus in the parking lot with its engine running. Noting several men wandering about, he decided to see if he might be able to target the traitor, although Pagano had doubtlessly attempted to alter his appearance. Boots parked beside a twenty-four-hour drugstore next door, took out a small pair of binoculars and swept the area. Remembering Pagano as a man of average height, he focused in on one figure that appeared about the right size. The man walked beside a taller companion.

Taking a closer look, he realized the strolling figure appeared a bit slimmer than the Pagano he remembered. That was something that could easily have been changed. The white hair fit, but he recalled a balding spot in front caused by a receding hairline. While considering this disparity, he picked up on something. The man's hair had been combed forward at an angle.

So it would cover a bald spot?

As he studied the face framed like a bullseye in the circle of the lenses, he knew it resembled Pagano in many ways. Yet, in others, he wasn't so sure. He hadn't seen the man in several years.

A person could alter a lot of things about himself, he reflected, but it would be difficult to hide peculiar mannerisms. He concentrated on recalling all he could about Pagano. Then it came to him. Pagano had an oddball grin, a sort of half-smile that pulled his mouth to one side as though his face were warped.

As he watched the man talk, the quirk showed up almost on cue. That same peculiar twist of the lips he remembered. Now he was certain. He had tracked down Pat Pagano, the traitor. Excitedly, he reached over and tapped his fingers atop the Congressional Medal of Honor case that lay on the seat beside him. It would be his war trophy.

Like any hunter, Boots was eager for the kill. So

eager, in fact, the passion it generated set off a totally unexpected reaction inside his overburdened body, something for which he was ill prepared. First came a return of that damnable pain in his chest. Then a growing numbness invaded his left arm. His jaw began to tingle. Something told him this was not just another irksome episode of angina.

Reaching for the cell phone on the seat beside him, he punched in the motel number and asked for Dom Locasio's room.

"Yeah?" Locasio answered in a laconic voice. He never bothered to say hello.

"Dom, this is Boots. I've found him." He spoke rapidly, his voice tinged with anxiety.

"Pagano?"

"Right. He's about to get on a red and white Nova Tours bus packed with senior citizens. It's at Lovely Lane United Methodist Church on Gallatin Road in Madison."

"Damn! Where are they headed?"

"New Orleans. I got a paper with times and all. They'll be on the Natchez Trace Parkway, spending the night at a Days Inn–"

His voice choked off as the searing pain suddenly intensified, almost like a knife jabbed into his chest.

"Where?" Locasio asked.

"Oh, God." Boots gasped, fighting to get his breath.

"What's wrong?"

"The heart...get an ambulance." Boots was sweating now. He reached a hand up to tug at his collar.

"Where are you?" The strain colored Locasio's voice.

"Drugstore...by the church parking lot."

"Lovely Lane Methodist? Hang on, Boots. I'll have somebody there pronto." Then the younger man apparently realized he was still missing a vital piece of information. "Wait. Where did you say they were spending the night?"

"Natchez." It was almost a whisper.

Boots dropped the phone. He needed air. If he could just open the door. Fresh, cool air. He reached over and pulled the door handle, then pushed against it with his foot. The exertion was too much. He fell back against the seat and fumbled with his collar. Sweat soaked his shirt.

Boots felt light-headed. Was this it? Was he cashing in his chips? His heart raced and the rushing blood pounded in his ears. He barely heard voices nearby.

"He must be having a heart attack," Fred said. He gazed over Bryce's shoulder.

Bryce's own heart had taken a jump in tempo as he stared at the burly figure sprawled across the car seat. He spotted the binoculars, the telephone.

They had found him.

"He's having trouble breathing. I know CPR." Fred pushed Bryce aside as he spoke, apparently believing his friend had been numbed by indecision. "Go call nine-one-one."

Save your executioner, Bryce thought? This man was clearly the enemy. Every bit as much as the Germans he had faced during the war. But did he really have any choice? If he refused to help, it would require a lot more explanation than he was prepared to give. And at the moment he was not sure just how badly his cover had been breached by the mob.

Displaying no emotion, Bryce nodded. "I'll alert them at the drugstore."

(End of Excerpt)

Order **Hellbound** from Amazon at
https://www.amazon.com/dp/0986162205

For an autographed copy, send a check for $15 plus $2 shipping and handling, along with signing instructions to:

Chester Campbell
8610 Sawyer Brown Road
Nashville, Tennessee 37221

www.ingramcontent.com/pod-product-compliance
Lightning Source LLC
Chambersburg PA
CBHW020653300426
44112CB00007B/366